SOCIAL WORK FACE TO FACE

To my parents

Social Work Face to Face

Clients' and social workers' perceptions of the content and outcomes of their meetings.

Stuart Rees

Edward Arnold

© Stuart Rees 1978
First published 1978 by
Edward Arnold (Publishers) Ltd
41 Bedford Square, London WC1B 3DQ

British Library Cataloguing in Publication Data

Rees, Stuart
  Social work face to face.
  1. Social case work – Great Britain
  I. Title
  361.3'0941   HV43

  ISBN 0–7131–6132–9
  ISBN 0–7131–6133–7   Pbk

Printed and bound in Great Britain at
The Camelot Press Ltd, Southampton

Contents

ABY 2309

Acknowledgements

This study could not have been carried out without the cooperation of many social workers. I am very grateful to those staff who were responsible for the cases whose progress I was able to follow closely. I was equally dependent on the interest and cooperation of clients and their families. I anticipated that obtaining people's agreement to being interviewed several times about current personal problems would be difficult. I was wrong. The clients' cooperation made interviewing relatively easy and always enjoyable. Alison Marr shared the interviewing with me. She communicated skilfully with both sets of respondents. Sandra Wood transcribed accurately and at great speed all the tape-recorded interviews. Mrs Marr and Mrs Wood were delightful colleagues. Their work was supported by a grant from the Social Science Research Council.

In the project's early stages I owed a great deal to the support and sharp criticism of Raymond Illsley. My colleagues, Phyllida Parsloe and David May, were always thorough and insightful in their observations regarding my early analysis of transcripts of interviews. Geoffrey Pearson's and Andy Rigby's constructive appraisal of the first draft was invaluable. I have heeded their advice. I owe a particular debt to the interest and friendship of Andy Rigby. His suggestions led to several improvements in the final manuscript. He is not responsible for any of the book's flaws. Len Hunt has helped me by always being prepared to discuss humorously and with insight both this research and related topics. In this respect the support of my wife, Ragnhild, was also invaluable. In several ways she is a co-author. She managed to ignore the incessant clatter of a typewriter, yet always found time to listen patiently to ideas which she had heard many times before. The final manuscript was typed by Mary Dinnie. She gave her time with characteristic generosity even though she had other, more pressing secretarial tasks. There are others whose names are not mentioned but with whom I have discussed social work face to face and on several occasions. I am grateful to them all.

STUART REES
Professor of Social Work, University of Sydney

Chapter 1

Politicians Making Plans

Alongside departments of social security, employment, health, education and housing, social-work agencies have become established as a part of most western countries' systems of social services. These agencies often report that they cannot meet the needs even of all those people who seek help. Why? Most social workers have received a lengthy training and most experience pleasant employment conditions. Yet they feel that their tasks are vague and vast and that some of their jobs should be performed by others. Why?

Many members of the public are reluctant to use the social-work agencies which have been established for their benefit. Why? What happens to those people who do bring their problems to the attention of social workers?

This book confronts these questions. Some social workers and their respective clients were asked to explain what was occurring in their face-to-face exchanges and what significance they attached to them in relation to other events in their lives. My objectives were to identify what social work meant to both sides and to unravel the circumstances associated with the clients' assessments of whether a social worker's intervention had helped them. These are aspects of social work which have remained largely undocumented.

The processes of interpretation and reinterpretation involved in the clients' and the social workers' several discussions about 'problems' and 'help' may sometimes seem trivial. But the image of social work which they portray collectively has wider significance than the details of any one encounter. These clients' experiences in their meetings with social workers were a test of some redirections in social policy and the challenges to the social workers which such changes provided. These meetings took place in the 1970s against a background of continuing debates in political, professional and administrative circles about the purpose of employing social workers and the most effective ways of doing so. The individual clients and social workers could hardly have remained unaffected by some of the consequences of those debates. The social workers had to make sense of some inconsistencies in policies affecting the delivery of social-work services. Cost-effectiveness arguments, for example, had contributed to the emergence of larger administrative areas yet a high value was still being placed on improving public access to services by decentralizing offices. Social workers were being asked to experiment in new ways to reach disadvantaged people but without any guarantee of growth in financial resources. Although some client groups were challenging professionals' autonomy, this was also a period which saw a mushrooming of social-work training courses and publicity about social workers' jobs in an increasing number of journals and newspapers. Social work was becoming big business.

In several countries in the 1970s, the persistence of some social problems was being attributed to the limited roles of various professionals (Cloward and Piven 1976), or to clients' behaviour (Ryan 1972). Areas of professional responsibility were increased. In Britain, local-authority social work was being financed by larger proportions of local taxes. Career opportunities for trained social workers were heightened and widened. The expansion and professionalization of social work were welcomed in the House of Commons and the House of Lords on the assumption that reorganization would benefit the public and allow social work to take its 'rightful place' alongside older professions (Hansard 1970, 729–53). At the American Council on Social Work Education's 1976 bicentennial conference, the keynote speaker, Congressman Flood, announced to delegates, 'You are striking a blow for social justice. You are today's revolutionaries.' The audience of educators had other concerns: the proliferation of other 'helping professions' and recent government cutbacks in the budgets allotted for social-work services. Conference controversies were not about some hoped-for new identity for an 'unloved profession' (Richan and Mendelsohn 1973) but concerned the respective merits of postgraduate versus undergraduate social-work training.[1]

Neither the attempts to tidy up social workers' official terms of reference nor any emphasis on achieving high standards in training could guarantee a matching of clients' expectations to social workers' interests and resources. On the contrary, new professional goals could divert attention from the needs of some client groups.

The publication of *Social Work and the Community* in 1966 and the

Seebohm Report in 1968 preceded the passing of the Social Work (Scotland) Act 1968 and, in England and Wales, the Local Authority Social Services Act, 1970. This legislation replaced separate services with amalgamated social-work and social-service departments, staffed by social workers accountable to team seniors, Directors and, ultimately, lay committees. Various hopes were held regarding the new departments' future achievements, including new partnerships with established voluntary organizations and with emerging self-help groups. Some commentators considered the Scottish legislation pioneering, others cautioned that its implementation depended on the resources and commitment of new Directors and their middle management.

No matter how much governments rearrange national systems of social-work services or agencies change their local policies, at the end of the day much of social work[2] boils down to an encounter between a social worker and a client or clients. Encompassing such interpersonal contexts are historical, legal and other events which merge and affect exchanges, in particular regarding clients' and social workers' interpretations of which problems are the responsibilities of which officials. In Scotland before 1969, services for children, the aged, the disabled and mentally handicapped, juvenile and adult offenders had developed piecemeal. Adults with difficulties which did not fall into these categories were not the official concern of local government, although voluntary organizations, such as Councils of Social Service, did exist to cater to needs outside the remit of statutory agencies.

Clients and social workers meet against a background not only of their immediate private interests but also of public issues regarding the organization and development of social work. A key issue in this study involved identifying how the social workers used their power to manage cases and the extent of the clients involvement in negotiations affecting their interests.

The social workers in this study, which ended in late 1974, were employed in two agencies in a Scottish city of approximately 200,000 people. One was a local authority department staffed by 50 basic-grade social workers, plus seniors and administrative staff. The other employed 11 caseworkers and derived its income from private as well as public sources. It will be referred to as 'the voluntary agency'. It had specialized in supporting single parents and families with multiple problems. Each agency's share of social work had been influenced more by the evolution of traditions than by explicit policy agreement. As an arm of government, the 'local authority' undertook work, such as completing social enquiry reports for adult courts, for which the voluntary agency was not responsible. In this respect the agencies' official functions were dissimilar. However, no attempt is made to compare their work, and cases involving compulsory supervision were not studied. Each organization was responsible for social work with a heterogeneous collection of people and problems. Each sent to the researcher details of cases which were 'new' in that the people concerned had never previously been allocated to a caseload. The 60 cases, studied from the time of first client/social worker meetings and up to at least six months later, involved 90 people 'seeking help' and 38 social workers.

Piecing together the content of these clients' meetings with their social workers, involved discovering the sort of knowledge which each took for granted, their expectations of one another and the criteria affecting the allocation of resources. Even the apparently simple task of discovering some of the conditions affecting the clients' access to social workers acted as a reminder that the meaning of social work could never be taken for granted. It varied both between clients and social workers and between different clients.

For example, one of the clients from the voluntary agency was a garage foreman. He was divorced and fighting a legal battle to regain custody of his children. He had little difficulty in dis-covering 'what this social work is about. You ask around and I can get away from work at any time.' The wife of a 60-year-old stroke victim was not so optimistic. 'I don't know what I'll do. I'm not able to go about. It's all new to me.' A senior administrator in the voluntary agency explained that because his agency was at the end of several bus routes and bordered a square which was always full of people, access should not be difficult. In addition 'Our signs ("marriage guidance council", "prisoners' aid") must give some idea of what we do. Our pamphlets in the Citizens Advice Bureau show that we've moved over from the days of giving blankets.' An elected councillor on the local authority's social work committee opposed advertising locally-administered disability benefits. 'You'd be flooded with requests. Worse than saying nothing. You'd never meet them.' A new social worker in the local-authority department doubted whether the high-rise building in which she and her colleagues had their offices would help their agency's professed open-door image. 'When I first came here I got totally lost. We're in such a remote corner, I think it must put people off.' It didn't put off the confident garage foreman but an old lady living alone required more than pamphlets or signs to discover services to make life less lonely or even warmer. Marooned on the third floor of a tenement, overlooking only a sombre backyard and beyond that a funeral parlour entrance, she preferred to gaze at her television and looked forward only to slow excursions to a corner shop. Social work to her was 'an allowance like security . . . I thought I'd get to hear of it if it was something for me.'

Some elaboration of this lady's and other clients' beliefs about social work, and regarding other experiences which had some bearing on their meetings with social workers, are the topics discussed in chapter 2. In chapter 3 the social workers discuss their occupation in general and the considerations which influenced their management of cases. In chapter 4 some of the topics referred to in the heretofore separate discussions of the clients' and the social workers' worlds reappear in their accounts of their several meetings. Through the use of case studies the social workers identify reasons for their decisions about their handling of a case. The clients evaluate whether they have been helped and what a social worker's intervention has meant to them. Chapter 5 summarizes those value judgements, which amounted to moral evaluations, which ultimately affected the social workers' decisions whether and how to intervene. Such calculations were most evident in the context of different client/social-worker relationships. However, they did not suddenly emerge there. They ran like a thread, providing coherence for the clients and the social workers. They cropped up in most clients' appraisals of themselves and their problems and in their anticipation of the criteria affecting people's entitlement to help from a social worker. They affected the social workers' selection of priorities and their ideologically based assumptions about their goals in particular cases.

Chapter 6 presents conclusions about the experiences of these clients and their respective social workers. It identifies some issues regarding the present training of social workers and suggests some policies regarding their future liaison with client groups. In an appendix, I have outlined my assumptions about this research and how it was carried out.

NOTES

1 This issue is a virtual American equivalent of the British Association of Social Workers' deliberations about the merits of having a professionally qualified social worker carry out simple tasks and the

need to develop another qualification for social workers who would carry out allegedly less sophisticated functions.
2 Leaving aside any discussion about the place of residential care and community work in 'social work'.

Chapter 2

Citizens Becoming Clients

In the past two decades British government reports have emphasized the desirability, in a democracy, of the need to increase people's involvement in matters which affect them. From Skeffington on planning to Seebohm on the social services, from Plowden on primary schools to Home Office prescriptions for the successful launching of community development projects, the value of client or consumer participation has acted as a beacon guiding civil servants and politicians to their conclusions. These, often offered as recommendations, talk of professionally-run services being sensitive to clients' needs. They refer to the need to change the balance of power between those who exercise it through knowledge or statute and those who traditionally have not had much influence over matters which affect them. With reference to the personal social services, if the values implicit in the notion 'participation' are to be taken seriously, people should at least be asked about their expectations of social work and the criteria they use to evaluate professionals' activities. Without information about these criteria, services may continue to be reorganized in ways which ignore conditions affecting public access; social-work educators will continue to articulate theories of intervention which are not based on empirical evidence and which are therefore likely to be unrelated to the ways in which people define their problems and seek help.

One axiom of social-work training refers to 'starting where the client is'. A corollary of this premise would stress the importance of learning about patterns of help-seeking behaviour in general as well as the problems of any one individual in particular. Included in such patterns would be variations in people's knowledge of a social worker's job. Although there have been several studies of people's perceptions of the terms of reference of staff in the personal social services and although these have identified certain common denominators in people's knowledge and beliefs (Glastonbury *et al.* 1973; Glampson *et al.* 1977), it is likely that there will be 'local' variations which will affect people's attitudes and expectations. For example, knowledge of social work may vary geographically as between Britain and North America, between different American states and Canadian provinces, or between Scotland and different parts of England and Wales. It may vary according to ethnic origin and the values associated with seeking help from an outside source. It may vary according to the life styles characterizing membership of different social classes. Even class distinctions, however, are too crude a criterion by which to distinguish some subtleties of help-seeking behaviour. For example, most of the people followed up in this study fell into classes 4 and 5 in the Registrar General's classification and could be dubbed 'working class'. But within such a category were very different people whose responses to apparently similar problems varied. Their expectations of authority and their style of coping with officials were not the same. Omitting to study such aspects of the clients' world would be to imply that potential help-seekers are an undifferentiated mass. They are not.

For each client and each social worker various other significant events preceded and followed their meetings with one another. Such face-to-face exchanges were related intimately to other experiences such as recent conversations with relatives, and the values and beliefs which had been built up over generations. A client's interview with a social worker lasted perhaps only an hour and in many cases was even shorter. One or two such exchanges were often the extent of these individuals' experiences of social work. What happened during the rest of the day, or during the remainder of that week, to affect an individual's interpretation of any recent meeting with a social worker or the possible significance of subsequent ones?

With a view to elaborating aspects of clients' experiences which seemed likely to affect their use of services, four topics will be discussed: the 'conditions' affecting people's access to social workers, including their knowledge and beliefs about agency functions; how they reached each agency and how their experiences *en route* might have affected their presentation of their request; how they anticipated the experience of becoming a client as illustrated by their feelings on being referred; some account of their past patterns of coping with others in positions of authority, differentiating one form of help-seeking behaviour from another. Before following these experiences we should know whom we are talking about. Who were the clients?

Who were the clients?

Following allocation of these 60 new cases, social workers were usually involved at first in meeting only one person. Overall, however, a total of 90 people were in some way involved as clients during or subsequent to these first meetings.

Other research has suggested that clients of social-service departments will be predominantly women, a large proportion of whom will be the heads of single-parent units or will be living alone (Goldberg and Neill 1972; Glampson and Goldberg 1976). My research confirms this. Of the 60 first clients, 41 were women and 19 men. In the age bracket 30 to 39, women out-numbered men by three to one. The percentage of people from broken family units – involving widowhood, separation or divorce – was three times the average for the total city population.

A striking two-thirds of the sample received all their income from supplementary benefit. In only 17 cases (28 per cent) was income derived from earnings. The sample included some people living on low wages and others living on pensions and savings. Although not exclusively poor and unemployed, these people received proportionately much lower incomes than the Scottish population as a whole (Social Trends, 1974).[1] Of 90 people who were of employable age, 43 (68 per cent) were unemployed. The high figure of unemployed was affected by the large number of women who were heads of single-parent families, by men who had no jobs because of temporary ill-health or permanent forms of disability and adults who were mentally handicapped.

The clients' ages ranged from 16 to 80. Young people under 16 were excluded. Eight clients (13 per cent) were under 20, 19 (32 per cent) and 17 (29 per cent) were in the age ranges 20 to 39 and 40 to 59. Sixteen people (26 per cent) were over 60.

This background information only hints at the sorts of 'requests' which were to be made to social workers. For example, the fact that a large proportion of people lived on low incomes did not show whether or how they managed, whether they sought help from relatives and/or from outsiders. Before discovering how these individuals fared in meeting some social workers, we should follow their pathways to such agencies. Some of these pathways were well signposted. Others were crooked and strewn with obstacles.

Accessibility

Access to personal social services depends partly on those agency employees who hinder one person at the reception desk or intake office but allow another person to pass through. However, all our client applicants had navigated beyond the gatekeeper receptionists and had met the social workers responsible for their case at least once. They had by-passed or overcome the controls exercised at 'the point of entry' (Hall 1974). But resources are rationed in other ways (Parker 1967). Agencies control access to social service goods by establishing explicit eligibility criteria and by the process of sifting, as operated by the implicit personal preferences of staff with responsibility for managing their own caseloads. For example the negotiations between social workers and clients depicted in this study will refer to the usually invisible and often unacknowledged practices of controlling access to resources through caseworkers' attraction to some people, slight interest in others and apparent indifference to some. Before that stage is reached and even before the obstacles at entry, other conditions affect how people meet social workers. These include recent incidents unconnected with social work, formative experiences of earlier years, such factors as geographical and physical obstacles and how an individual sees the connection between his difficulties and social workers' tasks. This might act as a trigger motivating him to seek help. It could have the opposite effect. Later in this chapter some individuals talk about the deterrent effect of the stigma which they associated with 'the welfare' in general rather than social work in particular.

Most parts of the city were well served by public transport, but there were other tangible resources affecting access to agencies. For example, in the 60 cases only 13 people had a telephone in their home and only eight owned a car. Seven of those who owned cars also had telephones. In terms of such useful aids to communication, most of these people and their families were therefore disadvantaged.

Voluntary agency staff had offices in their own self-contained building. Local authority social workers were housed in a multi-purpose office block which also contained employees of education, health, housing and recreation departments. These were some physical conditions affecting access. However, even if people live next door to an appropriate agency it is not necessarily 'accessible' to them. Some consider it their right to seek advice and assistance from doctors or lawyers, the citizens' advice bureau or social workers, teachers or the clergy, bank managers or stockbrokers. Others remain ignorant of the functions of such professionals or would not wish to trouble them. Cultural barriers such as lack of knowledge, coupled with a feeling that seeking help is inappropriate, impede access. This applies in other spheres of professional/client relationships such as medicine, education and means-tested welfare benefits (Arrow 1963; Jackson and Marsden 1972; Meacher 1973).

Clients' beliefs

Clients' were asked what 'social work' meant to them. In several instances the source of beliefs indicated that they had been held a long time and were related to salient past experiences. For example, an old man recalled that 60 years previously he had seen an old couple dispossessed of their belongings and taken off to what was then a workhouse for the aged and destitute. This building had since been converted into a geriatric hospital which he believed must be something to do with social work. Other beliefs about a social worker's job included a range of ideas from confessed ignorance to taken-for-granted assumptions, to what sounded like 'informed guessing'.

Prior to meeting a social worker, these people were unsure about their entitlement to consult such personnel and had no precise knowledge of what they did. None knew about the reorganization of local authority social work. Even those half-dozen people who had met pre-reorganization 'social workers', such as a probation officer and welfare officer, found the new all-purpose label confusing. A mother who visited what she thought was 'the health department' said,

> I didn't know what I could get help for. We just heard of the health department for getting Dad into a home and trying not to put him into the geriatric hospital . . . When I was waiting in her room there were phone calls and everything. I saw that it wasn't just putting Dad into homes.

Although respondents found 'social work' an imprecise term, many had known of the existence of the local authority or voluntary agency. The latter had existed for over one hundred years and had a sign outside which included the words 'Social Service'. Below the main sign was a smaller one saying 'Thrift Shop'. Activities in the shop were a separate part of the agency's work. To some people this sign was an historical symbol of 'social work' and as such a source of confusion.

Guesses about the voluntary agency's functions revealed local folklore and a legacy of ideas about the building and the activities of its staff. This organization was regarded as 'the welfare' or was associated with 'welfare', a concept with deep-seated connotations. Apart from those who 'didn't know', or 'hadn't given it much thought', clients assumed that it was a place where people went as a last, last resort after they had exhausted what they were entitled to from insurance-related or supplementary benefits in the social-security system. There were various illustrations of what was meant by welfare.

> I thought welfare was just for the down and outs. The sort of people who hang around down there.   (man of 49)

> I associated them (the voluntary organization) with the sort of Thrift Shop type. You know, the batchelor ladies doing their best to keep up the moral support of the community. But what they do has surprised me.   (man of 29)

Explanations of 'welfare' varied according to age and problems. Two elderly people had heard that the voluntary organization was a place where they might obtain coal. Families in financial difficulties thought they might get help with furniture or groceries. Several young mothers thought it was a place to obtain clothing for children. Money was seldom mentioned but people said they had heard the agency had been a source of financial help to others.

The assumption that this visible voluntary organization was a place for women not men, was expressed by three mothers. They had in mind that it was a woman's task to deal with financial and other domestic difficulties. A mother of three children who was in arrears with her rent said,

> I discussed the welfare with my friend, Rita. I never asked my man about them. He says the budgeting is my job.

This 'budgeting norm' and the 'for women only' assumption about social work derived from it was held only by some young mothers in financial difficulties who were asked about the agency's functions. But their beliefs were reinforced by the staff's practice of specializing in supporting unmarried mothers and single-parent families. Referring to her experience in that agency's waiting room another young woman said,

> When I went in there were three girls sitting in the waiting room. There was a chap outside and I just didn't expect to see a man. I thought it was all wives with their kids having problems. There is a girl along the road and I know she is under a social worker. I never thought I would see a man in there.

By comparison with the voluntary organization the local-authority department had no comparable history and was less visible. The existence of the building was known. It was obvious that it housed various officials but it was far from obvious that it contained social workers or what their precise functions were. There were fewer well developed ideas about the local-authority departments. The majority of those referred had not heard of 'social work' being there. They thought it was somewhere to go to get information such as that relating to housing, the registration of births, marriages or deaths.

In these respects the local-authority department was regarded vaguely as a place with authority where officials were employed to exercise a guardian-type role. Elaborating this point of view one man said he assumed that social workers were the same as health visitors, 'you know, those ladies in green who toddle in and toddle out again'. Old people thought the local-authority department was a place where people checked up on 'needy old people, the ones who fall down'. Some young families thought the agency checked to make sure children were properly looked after. Those who had never been dependent on supplementary benefits thought the local-authority department was 'the welfare', a place for those who were so badly off that they had to go there as a last resort. A young woman, recently separated from her husband, explained,

> My neighbour told me to go (to the social-work department) but I got the impression that if your house is all right, if you have got enough food in your cupboard, you are well enough off. They don't want to know you.

These blurred images originated from beliefs about the financial assessment function of government agencies. These were reactivated when clients recalled the connotation of agency titles. For example, two old-age pensioners discussed with one another whether the local-authority social-work department would be similar to the UAB, although the income maintenance agency of that name ceased to exist in 1940. Asked what they had known about social work several others, with and without experience of being assessed for entitlement to unearned benefits, lumped together social work and social security:

> The social security is a mystery, I would rather go without than go there. (Mother of 27, recently separated)

> Social workers gave me money but I don't know if it's a law of the land. When I tried to get clothes for Alice they wouldn't entertain me. (26 year-old mother)

The majority of respondents assumed that a social worker existed to help those who were younger or older than them or whose situation was worse than or different from their own. Those who referred to the voluntary agency's welfare functions had assumed previously that they were not the kind of person who would ever need to go into that building. Such 'social work' represented an aspect of life which they had hitherto not associated with themselves. Some hoped never to be financially dependent upon others and regarded obtaining such help as unpleasant. The values implicit in the notion of universally available social services were not taken for granted by most of this group. In their minds only selected bits of the world of the welfare state related to them.

Sources and routes of referral

Those who influence others in contacting a social worker are potential image makers. They can influence people's assumptions about agency functions, their views of themselves as possible clients and the general impression whether they and their problems will be taken seriously. The official who suggests casually that people should visit an agency but says nothing about it, often because he does not know himself (see Sainsbury 1975, 18–21), is likely to have a very different effect on people's attitudes than the person who gives detailed information and perhaps also follows up his referral. However, a recent summary of the effect which referral agents can have on the meaning of social work to the social-work client makes two generalizations. Firstly, irrespective of the source of referral it was safe to assume a general ignorance of social work and social workers. Secondly, when relatives and friends were instrumental in sending people to an agency, this personal network continued to be influential during the client's association with a social worker, often acting 'as a kind of Greek Chorus throughout the social-work action, commenting upon and sometimes – unlike a Chorus – influencing the outcome' (Timms and Timms 1977, 69). The most overlooked point about the importance of the referral system, assuming the social worker knows the identity of the referral agent, is its influence on that worker's interpretation of someone's problem and of his task in dealing with it. His impression of the urgency of someone's request can be influenced by his awareness of the possibility that some influential outsider may be checking later to assess what service was given.

Pathways to an agency are seldom incidental to what occurs between client and professional. They are part of the context of social work because they affect possibly one party's expectations of help *and* the other's initial reactions as to what can or should be done. This is the point to bear in mind. The actual details of which referral agents send which clients and under what circumstances are important not in isolation but as links in a chain of experiences. Sources and routes of referral often affect significantly an individual's interpretation of the purpose of a first meeting, the social worker's assessment of his task and the priority of his responsibility in any one case.

Although 'referral' is used to describe the process of people being sent by someone to someone, it is an ambiguous term which often fails to convey what was involved in reaching an agency and meeting an appropriate staff member. Regarding arrangements for first meetings, 'source of referral' means the person who, according to the client, was finally instrumental in his contacting a social worker or who, according to the social worker, influenced him in contacting the client. Sources of referral fell into ten categories (Table 2.1).

Table 2.1   Sources of referral

	No. of cases		Percentage
Health visitors	13	(2)*	22
Other social workers	10	(5)	17
Self-referral	8	(2)	13
Relatives	7	(4)	12
Local and central govt. 'officials'	6	(—)	10
Doctors	5	(—)	8
Neighbours or friends	4	(3)	7
Voluntary organizations	3	(—)	5
Police	2	(—)	3
Others (includes school Head-master (1) solicitor (1))	2	(1)	3
	60 (17)		100

* The figures in brackets refer to cases from the voluntary agency.

Most people were sent by employees of other city agencies. They had not referred themselves. Inter-agency collaboration also involved exchanges between social workers. For example, ten cases included eight referrals from hospital social workers and two from the local authority to the voluntary agency.

Only eight people were self-referred in that they had contacted the social worker of their own accord, without the push of an intermediary. Explaining self-referral, these people also mentioned their purpose in visiting the agency. They included two prospective parents, a couple who saw a local authority advertisement about heaters for the aged, an ex-prisoner seeking help with accommodation, a woman who wrote to 'the Council' about her handicapped child, parents who wanted 'the cruelty' to advise them about their son, a mother who had had previous contact with a probation officer and an old lady who saw the voluntary agency's sign above the Thrift Shop. The small number of self-referrals reflected obstacles affecting access, such as confusion about social workers' roles, people's assumptions that social work would not be anything to do with them and some individuals' feelings that seeking help from others was inappropriate.

Although these different sources were involved in referral, the link between what they said or wrote and how people reached the social workers was seldom direct. There was no consistency in the way professional employees arranged appointments. Some had fixed reasons for sending a person. With others it was a 'shot in the dark', a genuine but haphazard attempt to seek out some sort of help. Some referral agents' actions had the appearance of an attempt quickly to pass responsibility to somebody else, thus contributing to a shuttle service between one agency and another. From some sources people reached their destination quickly and comfortably, others got there after a longer ride by a more indirect route.

The term 'route' illustrates how referral agents influenced arrangements for first meetings. There were distinct routes of referral. 'Self-referral' was used if clients had consulted no other person immediately prior to telephoning, visiting or writing to a social worker. 'Uninformed' was used for those who had no prior knowledge of the referral agent's interest in bringing their circumstances to agency attention. 'Directed' was used when referral agents had both suggested a client should see a social worker and made arrangements for them to do so. 'Guided' was used when people received information or advice about seeing a social worker but no specific arrangements were made (Table 2.2.).

There was possibly a time lapse between an individual's recognition of some problem and his eventual meeting with some outsider. To what extent there was such a delay was not investigated. Most people reached social workers following the intervention of at least one intermediary. They did not seek out social workers of their own accord. In this respect the notion

Table 2.2   Routes of referral

Category	Source	No. of cases		Percentage
1. Self-referral	Self	8	(2)*	13
2. Uninformed	Health visitors	5		
	Doctors	3		
	Relatives	3	(2)	
	Housing department	2		
	Neighbours/friends	1	(1)	
	Other social workers	1		
	School	1		
		16	(3)	27
3. 'Directed'	Health visitors	5	(1)	
	Other social workers	4	(2)	
	Relatives	4	(2)	
	Police	2		
	Voluntary organizations	1		
	Doctor	1		
	Friends	1		
	Councillor	1		
		19	(5)	32
4. 'Guided'	Other social workers	5	(3)	
	Health visitors	3	(1)	
	Voluntary organizations	2		
	Friends	2	(2)	
	Housing department	1		
	Education dept.	1		
	Social-security offices	1		
	Doctor	1		
	Solicitor	1	(1)	
		17	(7)	28
	Totals	60	(17)	100

* The figures in brackets represent the numbers for the voluntary agency.

'seeking help' was not an apt description of the events leading to these first meetings. It would give a false impression to suggest that these individuals sought help from agencies without the involvement of others, or that different referral agents were consistent in the advice they gave or their manner of giving it. Potential clients would be referred from one of several sources each with different motives for influencing the possibility of a social worker's intervention. They might have different information or none. Some of the people who received information might never meet a social worker, might be lost *en route*. Some, such as these 60 individuals would be allocated eventually as cases.

Feelings about being referred

Individuals' reactions to the experiences associated with referral to a social worker will be very real to them even though others may not expect them to feel as they do. Each service user can elaborate the source of his feelings. Outsiders can't presume to know because there is no obvious connection even between the nature of someone's apparent predicament and their reactions to being brought to the attention of some agency. One aged and suddenly disabled person feels no stain on his name arising from his condition or from having to make it public by being referred to an outsider. Another feels a sense of stigma over admitting to any kind of dependence.

The meaning to individuals of being prospective social-work clients will be conditioned by relationships with family, friends and acquaintances. That generalization applies even though some people will want to keep secret any problems associated with their changed circumstances. Anticipating rejection they avoid interaction. Some individuals' harsh self-appraisal nullifies the effect even of the continued acceptance and reassurance of relatives or friends. The important consequences of others' treatment of potential clients are whether such 'people with problems' are enabled to feel integrated in the social life around them or segregated (Blaxter 1976, 1–15). The latter outcome could be the effect of policies implemented by professionals. It could result from the indifferent or even hostile attitudes of relatives. It could develop from a label which has been self-imposed.

Individual clients have hinted already[2] at the nature of their reactions to the business of being referred. The concern with being considered deserving was a common denominator in their otherwise unique management of and reactions to the circumstances of being unemployed and poor, to having become disabled, to being the parent of a mentally handicapped child, to having children who were allegedly beyond control, to the prospect of being an unmarried mother.

Asked whether it bothered them to be referred to a social worker, half of the sample said they felt neutral about it, the remainder that they experienced feelings of shame. This distinction does not portray groups of people entirely different in their reactions. Some replies reflected different interpretations of the question. Some people mentioned their feelings associated with meeting a social worker. Others stressed not so much the prospect of meeting this person, or even the route of referral, but the attitude towards them of family and friends. Some replies included comments about all these experiences.

(a) Neutrality

A majority of people in this neutral group were married and received their income from earnings-related benefits. Information from sources of referral suggested that the latter did not regard such people as having financial or other material difficulties. Only a small number of this group had had any recent experience of having their means assessed for income-maintenance purposes. Only four had experienced the break-up of their families through separation or divorce.

In expressing feelings of neutrality, respondents said that this experience did not make them feel ashamed or self-critical. They remained positive about their personal identity. Even the experience of being referred without prior knowledge had not affected them unduly. Their replies included examples of one of three things or a combination of them: they had no previous experience of unhelpful officials; irrespective of different reasons for contacting a social worker they felt they had nothing to hide from that person, often because discussions with someone else had neutralized any sense of shame; thirdly, for a few people the experience of having to meet officials was not unusual, they felt they knew what meeting a 'social worker' would be like.

Some pensioners replied that they had never given this topic any thought, that thinking about 'that sort of thing' would be too much. Those who viewed the prospect of meeting a social worker as of little consequence qualified this by stressing their anxiety about any first meeting with any 'official'.

In six cases which sources of referral defined as involving requests for aids for old people, the latter said they were not troubled about the matter because they did not expect to have to do or say much. When they met the social worker she had not only been pleasant but had confirmed their expectations. Recalling the referral, each said he did not mind and some that they had welcomed the prospect of mentioning what had previously been private information, known only to themselves.

Younger people had been reassured by what they had heard. For example, a mother referred on grounds that a doctor suspected that her young child was mentally retarded and would require special nursery schooling, spoke of a conversation with an acquaintance.

> My neighbour told me 'they could do anything for you, they help people'. I used to talk about things with the welfare lassie (a health visitor). She didn't tell me about a social worker but she was helpful.

In some cases, feelings about being referred reflected relatives' responses to situations affecting family relationships. In each instance the clients did not regard this referral as implying their failure. For example, in cases relating to the control of children, the respective parents regarded this event as an attempt to enlist the help of someone with authority, an experience which did not trouble them, although it may have bothered the children. A father explained that he thought the alternative to not getting advice from such a source was that his son would be in more trouble. He was prepared to give any interested outsider a chance to prove himself as long as he could talk to them in confidence and they would 'put sense' into his son.

The reaction of family members provided important re-assurance that the circumstances surrounding referral were neither exceptional nor blameworthy. For example, one un-married mother had not been made to feel that her reputation in the eyes of her family had changed. They treated her as they always did. They had not made her feel that there was any psychological price to pay for giving birth to her child or for keeping him.

Although previously they had not met anyone dubbed social worker, there were families who had been long-term unemployed and others who had brought up mentally and physically handicapped children. The former had had previous encounters with officials such as supplementary benefits officers and were blasé about the prospects of meeting someone else, although fathers said they had been rebuffed by 'security officials' on previous occasions and did not expect much help on this.

Families who had brought up handicapped children recalled previous contacts with representatives of voluntary organizations such as the Red Cross, with local authority personnel and doctors. Irrespective of whether they felt they knew about social workers, they regarded the business of meeting this person as nothing new. However unique they had once regarded their child's handicap, they had even recently seen and heard of other families with handicapped children and been reminded that there was nothing unusual about their circumstances. The mother of a mentally handicapped teenager explained,

Over the years whenever we've moved we've contacted centres for handicapped children. We weren't too troubled this time because before, even when we couldn't get an attendance allowance – she needs attention all the time, I can't leave her at all – we had seen children on 'Nationwide' who couldn't get it and who had to be carried, who were a thousand times worse than Gloria.

(b) Shame

The majority of the 35 people (58 per cent) who had said that it bothered them to be referred were single, widowed, divorced or separated and received all or part of their income in supplementary benefit. Some illustrated other aspects of their circumstances, such as the desertion of relatives, which had coloured their expectations of 'social work'. Some referred to immediate events, others to value premises held for a lifetime.

A dictionary definition of shame refers to a 'feeling of humiliation excited by consciousness of guilt or shortcoming, of having made oneself or been made ridiculous, or of having offended against propriety, modesty or decency' and also to the 'restraints imposed by shame'. A psychoanalytically oriented definition refers firstly to an infantile emotion experienced as a result of exposing oneself prematurely and foolishly. That author also discusses the link between shame and doubt, stressing the (often secret) fears which threaten an individual's consciousness, making it difficult at important stages of life for that person to make a new beginning (Erikson 1968).

Not all respondents mentioned all these dimensions of the meaning of shame. Some regarded themselves as discredited in their own eyes. Others said they were being treated as shameful by others irrespective of how they felt themselves. In practice this distinction merged. People mentioned the peculiarity of their present circumstances and how their self-appraisal had been affected by the reactions of others. These reactions reminded them of unpleasant past experiences and their own critical attitudes to users of 'welfare services', a predicament not too dissimilar from their current one. In these respects there were almost as many reasons for 'feeling bothered' as there were respondents. Overlapping occurred in references to the value of independence, as in beliefs about desirable personal attributes and the respectability of family status, stress on the importance of maintaining financial independence, or by reference to both circumstances. Independence was valued by some because it meant keeping away from other people for the time being. But the circumstances surrounding referral made such privacy and confidentiality difficult to maintain. For example, 11 people were adjusting to the prospect of having just become the heads of single-parent families. Each saw themselves being forced into some temporary dependence on others. In consequence they anticipated that they would have to reveal certain aspects of their situation which might have remained hidden if their family status had not changed.

These individuals' assumptions about social work, plus the rejection and prejudices of relatives gave them a feeling of powerlessness. A man of 30 explained,

> My mother's attitude was that it was a disgrace to have the family breaking up, so I shouldn't think of going anywhere.

A mother of two children and recently separated recalled,

> The situation with me was you felt things were really at rock bottom and you will go and stick your head in the oven. You'd never be like that, I don't think, if people sort of knew that social workers were available.

Such powerlessness was also explained by women who said that in their recently changed circumstances there was little they could do except restrict contacts with people who might know them or know about them. Girls living in a mother-and-baby home explained that to avoid being seen as 'the girls from the home' they never caught a bus from the nearest bus stop but walked in another direction, taking a bus at another stop on a less obvious route into town.

Several expressed shame in terms of their sense of isolation and fear. A young woman described how she was lying in hospital waiting for the birth of her baby.

> I did not want to see anybody. It was just my pride. My sister told me 'You can't come back here'. I thought that I had to go and ask for help. It was that that I didn't want to do. I thought if my family wouldn't help me why should I go and face a stranger. I just sat in the ward and thought, 'My goodness, wait till she comes along'.

Some believed that being sent to a social worker could have unpleasant consequences. They suspected that they might not be kindly received or have their affairs dealt with confidentially. A mother of eighteen said,

> Being quite honest I thought they would take my children from me because I was an unmarried mother. I remember someone from the welfare took my cousin's children away years ago when I was a child myself. I have never forgotten this.

The heads of broken families made similar comments. A mother aged 34,

> Well, I was terrified when I knew he was coming the first time . . . just terrified. I said, 'Here is a man coming to see me about the children.

What is he going to do?' I suppose it's just a natural thing on your mind.

The social base of the sense of shame felt by single parents included both their preliminary moral judgement of themselves *and* references to their treatment by family intimates (Finer 1974, 214; Goffman 1968). Others spoke more specifically of their appraisal of themselves as potential recipients of 'help'. They mentioned values which they considered it desirable to adhere to but deviant to ignore; they stressed pride in previous financial independence and what they saw as the undesirable social implications of being unable to manage alone, even temporarily. Such feelings were expressed in particular by elderly people who had retired from full-time employment and by widows. Explanations of being bothered included comments like that of a woman recently widowed,

> I am the independent type whether I should be or shouldn't. I have always been the type that liked value for money and I just don't want money that I haven't earned.

This small number of older people had been taught that asking help from others was a sign of weakness. A married woman aged 76:

> My father was a good worker. My mother was a good worker. They were both good living. We were taught to be what we should be. We were churchgoers and things like that. No, we don't like asking for help. We led a quiet, sedate life, no outings at any time.

Another pensioner said,

> I haven't liked to tell my husband about this and I wouldn't even like to mention the friend who said where to go.

Pride in independence was also mentioned in the context of references to the disreputable behaviour of others who used 'welfare services', those who, by these individuals' reckoning, were less entitled to 'help' than they were. At least 15 of these people discussed their feelings in terms of distinctions between deserving and non-deserving groups. They considered themselves deserving. One woman mentioned that her husband had always paid his taxes, another that her husband had fought for his country.

People in this group engaged in a circular logic. If welfare was the same as, or worse than, being dependent on unearned benefits and if social work was associated with welfare, it followed that the business of seeking help from that source was related to previous unpleasant experiences which they wanted to denounce and avoid. Such experiences at supplementary benefits offices were easily recalled:

> I don't like their attitude, it's a horrible place. I don't like going there, it's terrible the way they treat people.   (A widow of 50)

You are treated like a beggar there; you sit for hours.   (A widow of
    63)
These people were in a dilemma. They had grounds for thinking
that visiting this agency would involve the risks of being turned
down, of being treated in a shameful way by not receiving the
attention they deserved. Yet they wanted to emphasize their good
reputation. In a normal run of events people like themselves did
not go to such officials or places. Such agencies were frequented
by the non-deserving poor, those who got help because of
dishonourable ploys and disreputable circumstances. They had in
mind certain negative reference groups, 'the winos' and 'down-
and-outs' whose alleged misbehaviour they did not wish to think
of emulating. The contention that they were deserving, not
undeserving, represented efforts to preserve some sense of
respectability, to protect themselves from the contaminating status
of being a typical client of 'the welfare'. Their explanations were
peppered with examples of someone whom they 'knew' or
assumed received help from 'the welfare'. A woman of 63:

My neighbours, they got a rent rebate, yet he's 16 stone something.
People like him can go up and they never work. They never want –
that's what gets me.

The same person went on to say that the Queen, although
obviously not poor, was not deserving,

There was one time when I was without help for a couple of weeks.
My book didn't come through. I know when it was – the Queen's
anniversary, that's right. She was sitting there 'tight' and I had
nothing. A great big feed in front of her. I said 'look at her and I have
nothing in the house'.

Another widow:

There's a family just down from me, they can get everything. They
destroy their house, they are like an eel but they say they get things
because they've got asthma. Well, I've got asthma and I can't run
about like them.

A man of 49, one of those who assumed social workers were 'the
welfare', had recently lost his job and was facing financial
dependency for the first time. He felt ashamed because he believed
that respectable people would not go to such agencies.

Those who emphasized the distinction between deserving and
non-deserving people, had had what they regarded as unpleasant
and even humiliating experiences regarding applications for
financial help. Those who had not had such experiences in
meetings with officials regarded themselves as deserving but not
in relation to other undeserving groups. They gave other
explanations of strong feelings about the prospect of being

interviewed by social workers. For example, one woman said that she and her husband had always worked hard. She mentioned how they had cherished their independence. When faced suddenly with the debilitating illness of her husband she assumed,

> We'll get everything we deserve. We have never in the past had to ask help from any of these welfare people. We have never needed help till Dad's legs gave way.

Orientations to seeking help

In introducing 'the clients' world', I mentioned 'help-seeking behaviour'. This concept was intended to emphasize that different people respond differently to those whose job is to assess needs and give assistance. If people can't solve difficulties with the aid of family or friends, they may make use of outside agencies. But they make use of outsiders such as social workers, in different ways. Their manner of 'making use' requires examination.

It is important to ask how many clients had talked over their problems with their relatives before consulting a social worker or being sent to one, and the effect of such consultation. But this topic is marginal to the objective of exploring some consequences of these clients' previous experiences of seeking help and coping with officials.

Twenty-five people had consulted relatives and friends about the matter which led to their seeing a social worker. A proportion of these had relatives in a similar predicament to themselves and had not found such consultations helpful. Such relatives were powerless to do much except reinforce a way of life in general and blurred images of the helping professions in particular. The remainder of the sample, including six who had no relatives available, had not consulted family members. One of three reasons or a combination of them was given. Firstly, breakdown in relationships between family members provided the occasion if not the reason for being referred. For example, a girl of fifteen had run away from home after years of family strife. Secondly, some people felt ashamed about their predicament and feared a judgemental reaction from family members. Thirdly, some people wanted confidential information and the advice which they assumed only a professional outsider could provide. For example, people with accommodation difficulties such as over-crowding in a relative's home, had not discussed their concern because the resources to deal with it could only be provided by some outsider.

In addition to relationships with relatives and friends, these people had had experience of coping with other adults, in particular people in positions of authority such as parents, teachers, doctors, policemen and landlords, social security personnel or social workers. These associations influenced norms and values which in turn affected how they defined problems and sought help. There were consistencies in their ways of defining problems, seeking help and responding to social workers and other officials. The concept 'orientation' will be used to refer to these consistencies, to behaviour patterns in seeking help and managing such relationships.

When the research began no such concept was in mind. It merely seemed probable that past experiences provided a frame of reference to influence the conduct which people considered most profitable or appropriate in meeting social workers. In a search for clues regarding such connections, three general areas were explored.

1 How had individuals responded to the authority of others now and in the past?
2 Had they been in the habit of discussing problems and ways of dealing with them with family members?
3 Had they been in the habit of planning the management of their domestic affairs?

In addition to analysing tape-recorded answers to these questions, clients were observed as they recounted their reactions to particular officials' written communications, as in a summons to appear in court, to visit a headmaster, to appear before children's panels and in demand notices from clothing clubs. Some were also observed in their interviews with social workers, social-security officers and in a court. The correspondence between observations and clients' answers to these questions provided information on which to base a classification of orientations as in the following table. This was not preconceived to test and predict behaviour. It evolved from the research and is used as a means of describing the content of and the distinctions between three orientations: passive; assertive; circumspect (Table 2.3).

Because the purpose was to obtain some 'measure' of clients' responses to the authority and potential helpfulness of outsiders, emphasis was placed on one criterion. For example, people in the passive group said they usually accepted (even if they resented or subsequently disagreed with) the authority of others. Those in the assertive and circumspect groups said that they had and would challenge the authority of others. Such acceptance and challenge took various forms and these will be discussed.

Table 2.3 Classification of orientations

	Criterion	Related behaviour	
Orientation	Had challenged authority	Discussed/analysed difficulties	Had planned events
Passive	No	No	No
Assertive	Yes	Yes/No	Yes/No
Circumspect	Yes	Yes	Yes/No

The table shows the main trends in respondents' answers but there was overlap between one orientation and another. This overlap suggests inconsistencies in my description of orientations. This issue is important. It requires elaboration. Orientation refers not to personality traits but to patterns of problem-solving behaviour as evidenced by adaptations to and interaction with officials. Two points should clarify this. Firstly, apart from different reactions to those in positions of authority, in other respects clients' behaviour was often similar. For example, some of the passive group said that there had been occasions when they tried to discuss difficulties with family members. The account of circumspect orientation includes examples of people who said they usually planned ahead but were not always in a position to do so. The most obvious differences were between the passive and assertive orientations on the one hand and the circumspect on the other. The latter behaviour had developed from individuals' experiences of learning how some officials' performance of their jobs affected other people's lives and how, in meetings with officials, ordinary citizens could represent their interests effectively. The assertive and passive orientations had developed from some individuals' relative ignorance of the power of institutions, such as schools, departments of housing, employment and social security, a reluctance to use them and a history of unsuccessful encounters with officials. My second point is this. Although in each case there was evidence of some consistency in matters of problem solving, I am not implying that such orientations were permanent. Consistencies facilitate explanations. However, each person's orientation might shift, not only according to the problem and the official whom they are dealing with, but also when other circumstances change, as when people get older and lose relatives, when they gain or lose jobs. That hypothesis was not investigated.

Passive orientation

Passive orientation refers to people's uncomplaining acceptance of their circumstances as illustrated by the feelings that they had no entitlements to 'help', that their circumstances would either remain the same or get worse. When faced with officials and officialdom such individuals were reluctant to be advocates for themselves.

Many people contended that they were not in the habit of openly questioning the points of view of those in positions of authority. Such a response was characteristic of three groups, the poor, the old who might also be poor and those young people whose experience in their schools and homes was that to avoid conflict the most sensible response to people with authority was to flee, or at least not to disagree openly.

The majority of people in this passive grouping were long-term dependents on supplementary benefit. It included only seven who were employed. Others of employable age included twelve single women, three widows and nine heads of single-parent families. Many had relatives in similar financial circumstances as themselves.

All the clients in this group could give examples of occasions when they had experienced fear and confusion in the face of officials, such as social-security personnel in the case of poor families; police, teachers and sometimes parents in the case of young people, a generalized respect for 'them' in the case of old people. Such individuals may have behaved in an authoritarian way at home but in response to 'officials' they were submissive. Their image of social order was that it had not been and was not likely to be kind to them and in the face of present and future difficulties, the least distressing or most appropriate adjustment was to put up with what came.

An example of what such passiveness might involve if an individual left familiar surroundings and was obliged to meet officials, occurred in the case of 48-year-old Mr Kapes.[4] He had been brought before a traffic court for having an unlicensed car outside his home, although the vehicle was dilapidated and broken down. The social worker was in contact with the family but did not know of the court visit. Mr Kapes was unrepresented and described how he had been anxious to please the court. Asked by the sheriff whether he could pay £5 a week off a fine of £30 with £10 costs, he readily agreed even though he was in considerable rent arrears, owed money to credit collectors, had five children and was supported only by supplementary benefits.

No one was there for me. It was all over quickly. I said what money
we had and he worked it out. 'I think you can pay so much a week,'
he said. I said, 'Yes, sir, I'll be doing my best, I can manage that.'

Eight months later, beset with several debts, he had not paid a
penny of his fine and was being threatened with imprisonment.

Mr Kapes's submissiveness in this and other similar, brief
encounters had developed partly from the way in which financially
dependent people like himself had been assessed and processed by
various officials. A feature of Mr Kapes's passive response was that
he did not expect people to be able to help him. He always
appeared to comply with the demands of others although in his
own home he asserted himself over his wife and children,
sometimes by uncompromising physical means.

A disproportionate number of old people were concerned with
'correct behaviour', with being polite and submissive to people in
authority. Many showed an almost feudal deference to officials and
seemed to assume that what was being done or not done on their
behalf was not only 'correct' but represented the limit of what was
possible. They showed anxiety at the prospects of meeting officials,
an undue reticence in negotiations. Visited by the researcher at the
time of the first interview, two couples had carefully laid ready
their rent and pension books, assuming that the researcher would
want to inspect them.

One old lady spoke of her fear of the medical profession and a
similar reluctance to seek a social worker's help.

I have been in hospital lots of times. I've never seen anybody like an
almoner. I'm frightened to ask about anything in there. I feel I
shouldn't. I mean because I know if they are taking me into hospital
they have either to kill you or cure you. That's what they are there
for.

The same woman had wanted to send the researcher a Christmas
card prior to his expected second visit but her husband had said,
'you can't do that sort of thing'.

He said I had no business to do that, what would your wife think if I
did that? He said, 'You'd best keep yourself to yourself and wait to
see if he comes.'

'Keeping themselves to themselves' is virtually the motto of people
who do not expect much, whose perception of social inequality is
based on assumptions about a hierarchy of status and who have
been frustrated in past attempts to obtain help, particularly with
regard to claims to social security and other benefits. This point
about the consequences of previous unsuccessful or unpleasant
attempts to obtain financial assistance applies to people of all ages.
But it seems that the older people get, the more likely it is that such

experiences reinforce their expectations of how they should respond to people with authority and the models of social order which they already hold. For example, a widow of 68 explained:

> My trouble is I just dress nice and respectable. I put the pennies by and I've got myself a new coat from the sales. Once my electricity was cut off for three and a half months and I just sobbed when the Assistance man came. He said there was nothing more to do to help. I said that was all right, he wasn't to worry. He said he thought there was a place I could go for my nerves.

Sometimes this tendency to agree with others if they had to but generally to try to keep themselves to themselves, meant not only that people did not trouble officials but also that they didn't want to 'cause difficulty' within their own family. A widow aged 77 said,

> My stepdaughter tries to help me but she has enough to do with her own family and I don't like bothering anybody else with my problems. I wouldn't tell any of my friends and neighbours, I like to keep myself to myself.

Assertive orientation

This orientation was characterized by those who said that they did not passively accept their lot, that they were not overawed by the authority of officials, that they had asserted themselves in order to disagree with the point of view of some outsider, or to gain publicity or redress for a sense of grievance. Each of these individuals had either

1 Shopped around for help, and/or
2 Written letters to newspapers, the Queen or the Prime Minister, and/or
3 Made 'complaints' either to doctors, a lawyer, a councillor or social worker.

Although the majority of the sample were women, the majority of 'first clients' in this group were men. They had some experience of meeting outsiders, whether in employment, as a result of previous imprisonment, trade-union membership, attempts to obtain work or State benefits. Compared with those showing a passive orientation they had more experience of managing relationships in public.

Rather than acquiesce passively to the demands of outsiders, accept those people's lack of interest in them, or their own sense of discomfort, these people at some time or other reacted in the ways mentioned. In so doing they retained some sense of identity in the struggle with authority. It was 'them' against 'us'. Their efforts had seldom resulted in any changes in circumstances. They had confirmed their expectations that the business of meeting with officials would be frustrating if not a waste of time.

Several described aspects of their past as miserable, yet they responded to present difficulties with anger rather than resignation. In terms of family life or employment, housing conditions or health, few had had sufficiently consistent good experiences which might have fostered more optimistic feelings. Describing why there were no relatives with whom he could discuss things, or why he and his family felt isolated, Mr Day said,

> I was illegitimate. My mother was from Doomburgh so they sent her to Liverpool to have me. They had to hush things up when I came back here for my boyhood. I may have relatives in Doomburgh but basically nobody wanted me.

Three sets of circumstances encouraged and provoked these individuals' assertiveness:

1 A feeling of confusion about the relationship between the functions of various officials and their (the clients') difficulties.
2 A sense of confusion and frustration about social security entitlements.
3 A sense of grievance at being wrongly or poorly treated by people with official positions.

These conditions can be illustrated in the case of Mr Hay. He had been a trade-union member most of his life and had been declared unfit following an accident at work. He was bitter with his employers for their alleged shabby treatment which included the offer of a small pension or lump sum payment of £168 together with a plaque which merely thanked him for his twenty-nine years' service. He was in occasional contact with a general practitioner, a consultant physician, a lawyer, a social worker, social-security and housing-department officials. His efforts to represent his own interests were usually thwarted. This happened because the assertiveness of a man with few other personal resources appeared either not to have been taken seriously, or to have been labelled 'troublemaker' by various officials. For example, he complained that he had been refused legal aid in a civil matter and that the solicitor concerned had tried to avoid either seeing him or giving an explanation. To verify this story the researcher interviewed the lawyer. That person acknowledged that Mr Hay could represent himself 'reasonably well', but that he considered that he could not maintain this apparent reasonableness. The lawyer said,

> He takes a pride in himself. He knows how to use the telephone. He usually makes appointments to come and see me and he is always well dressed and well turned out. He seems intelligent and articulate

at least until he gets on his hobby horse. I made some enquiries at the Corporation where he works. People there said he was something of a troublemaker. He often tried to fight other people's cases as well as his own.

Secondly, with regard to financial entitlements, Mr Hay was confronted with what he regarded as a bewildering array of conditions. He received a small pension from his job but this was no asset because it resulted in a reduction of supplementary benefit. He explained that if this had been a war-disability pension he would not have been disqualified from maximum entitlement to other benefits. He had received 30p a week, eventually increased to 45p as a supplement to help with his rent. The disablement resettlement officer advised him to refuse this in order to qualify for a local authority rent rebate. At the 'labour exchange' he had been advised to sign on as a disabled person. He considered that this restricted his choice of jobs and placed him in a status which he resented. According to his calculations he and his wife had overpaid £9 to a clothing company and when they pointed this out they had merely received a circular letter threatening to take him to court. The company subsequently admitted their mistake.

Such a person felt victimized, without contacts, without support, without someone who understood his point of view. How could he explain it?

> I found out that if you were a member of the Freemasons you have no trouble getting jobs with the 'town'. If you don't have any contact with them you've had it, you are on the heap. The Freemasons just look after their own.

His assumption that only the non-deserving got help was being confirmed because his was a 'deserving case' and look what had happened to him.

> I was brought up to hate charity, to learn to stand on your own two feet, not to ask for things if you could solve them yourself. I have had so many let downs I don't want to go any more. Either no one seems interested or no one knows about it. The only thing left to me now is to take this thing to the Press.

Mr Hay went to the local paper. To demonstrate that his word was reliable he produced a letter on headed notepaper acknowledging his participation in the first part of the research. The newspaper representative, a reporter, was suspicious and telephoned the researcher to ask whether this man's story was authentic. Later the newspaper published Mr Hay's photograph and a full-page article about his circumstances.

Others had also written to papers and had had articles published about their circumstances. The Day family were featured in a

Sunday newspaper article, 'They do their homework by candlelight'. They unashamedly published their hardships although this resulted not in any change of circumstances but usually more advice, and sometimes abuse, in letters from readers' columns.

The two clients referred to above explained aspects of their past which prompted their unwillingness merely to put up with things. Mr Day said,

> I don't want to be under officials for ever. I want to deal with my life but we get depressed. In the end we usually say to one another 'bugger the in-between, let's go to the top', that's why we wrote to the Prime Minister.

Mr Hay reflected,

> My father was a cooper, a strict and loyal Conservative even though he worked under terrible conditions and it never did him any good. I don't see quite so much why I should be pushed around.

Circumspect orientation
Circumspect means 'wary, cautious, taking everything into account'. In their experience of contacting officials, people described as being circumspect in orientation showed evidence of what might be termed certain 'citizen skills'. My use of the word refers to

1 Assumptions that though they lacked precise knowledge about agencies' terms of reference they could obtain such information and use it to enhance their chances of obtaining a service.
2 Awareness that when meeting people in positions of authority they were involved in negotiations and had knowledge of how they might influence decisions in their favour.
3 Expectations of officials and officialdom which were more optimistic than the other two groups already described.

These individuals had a sense of security which was derived from income, or the status associated with having a regular job and/or the support of relatives or friends and the consequent sense of belonging. All had relatives available and eight out of fourteen had talked to relatives about their visit to the social work agency. Five of the six who had not done so were among those who maintained that they were well able to manage this particular request or 'trouble' without contacting family members.

These people maintained that they did not go out of their way to avoid meeting people in positions of authority and they were usually confident in making such contacts. They regarded themselves as able to represent their interest directly, or with the help of relatives such as sons and daughters. They had notions of how they might get things done. They not only felt able to assert themselves when necessary, they also expected to be able to do so in a manner which would benefit them.

The daughter-in-law of a man of 80 talked of her assumptions and experiences regarding officials concerned with the care of the elderly.

> I feel services are there just for the asking – if you treat those people as you would like to be treated yourself. There's never any use being nasty about anything.

She was referring to her first interview with a social worker during which she learned what was involved in obtaining accommodation for elderly people and left assured that her request would be properly investigated. Contrast her reactions with those of people who had also asserted themselves by enquiries about entitlements but with different results. Mr Day, referred to earlier, said,

> I tell you I've been insulted by almost all the 'social workers' in the County. They didn't seem to care about us but just told us what we couldn't get.

Those who were passive in orientation mentioned the value of maintaining their independence by keeping themselves to themselves. More circumspect people explained that if necessary they could maintain their independence by making selective use of officials. This difference reflects contrasts in confidence and self-respect between the two groups. The latter included those who expected to be able to get things done, if necessary by going to the top and trying to manipulate. For example, when faced with the task of finding day-care accommodation for his mentally handicapped daughter a father with a white-collar job had telephoned the medical superintendent for the region and asked him to intervene on his behalf. Describing her attitude to the business of seeking help, a journalist said that she and her husband would know where to go because they were 'in that line of business'. In the past she had noticed that people unable to stick up for themselves were often poorly treated, whereas those with more confidence and assertiveness fared better at the hands of professionals. She recalled that ten years previously she had had a baby and had been in a mother-and-baby home.

> I had a Guild of Service who dealt with the adoptions. It was a Miss Dean. She was always very pleasant to me but not to some of the other girls. She was of the old school but if you stood up for yourself you were alright. Some of the younger girls of fifteen or sixteen were the ones who really needed sympathy. She used to be very harsh on

them and tell them that they were going to do this and they didn't have the common sense to turn around and say 'but I don't want to do it'.

'Circumspect' is a label of experience, an indication of what has happened in the past, a reference to a form of behaviour likely to be repeated. This group had certain 'citizen skills' which could be an advantage in meetings with professionals because such an orientation was often welcomed by staff. They liked involvement with someone whom they sensed 'spoke the same language'. These clients' reactions to their difficulties were perceived by the professionals concerned as not inappropriate responses. For example, a social worker described meeting the mother of a mentally handicapped six-year-old.

> I think she was healthily aggressive. I learned a long time ago that you have to be able to take a great deal of aggression from parents of handicapped children.

Contrast this comment with that of the lawyer in the case of Mr Hay. In a situation of conflict, in which that man was seeking legal aid and demanding an explanation as to why he had been turned down previously, the solicitor said he had heard that the client's aggressiveness was troublesome. It was anything but 'healthy'.

On occasions, the recognition that people may be able to help themselves will enable a social worker to feel justified in limiting involvement. Referring to the family whose father visited the local authority following his telephone call to a consultant physician-in-charge of services for the mentally handicapped, the social worker observed,

> They are more coping than some families in their understanding of the problem. They know where to go for information. They have contacts which a lot of people wouldn't have. They've made use of them and they've been able to say 'we've found ourselves a better service than you were able to provide'. That's unusual.

People with some 'citizen skills' had not always received treatment which matched their general optimism. Much depended on the resources, ideology and style of the relevant professionals. Some individuals recalled meetings at which officials had not been helpful. But the client's persistence had apparently brought results. A Miss O. aged 35 referred to an 'unhelpful' medical social worker,

> She muddled me up too much and I told her this. She told me I had left work two weeks too early. I had a great palaver getting any maternity allowance. I had to keep getting sick lines from the doctor so that I could have an income. . . . It took me a long time to sort that out.

The style of coping with difficulties was self-reinforcing. Those who were passive in orientation had seldom had helpful experiences to make them more hopeful. Regarding their meetings with outsiders they tended to feel powerless, pessimistic and resigned. Those who were assertive in orientation had often had meetings with officials which had seldom resulted in improvements. These experiences fostered a resolve to shop around more agencies, including the press, usually in vain. They had a sense of grievance but remained powerless in spite of their anger. Those who behaved more circumspectly had experienced relationships which enabled them to meet officials expecting to be well treated, to be able to influence any required change in their circumstances. They had a greater sense of control, felt more confident and hopeful.

Summary

Clients' relative ignorance of social work affected their access to these and related services. A system which was not known to exist did not exist. This applies to potential clients and to others who could be instrumental in people meeting social workers. In the experience of several clients the ignorance of social work among some referral agents – teachers, doctors, a lawyer as well as relatives – was not only woeful but also wilful: rather than finding out, it was easier to stereotype social work as something to do with people who had not been successful, who in some way were deviant.

Fulfilling social-work tasks usually involves some cooperation with other agencies. It is not surprising therefore that potential clients' perceptions of social work should include their views of bureaucracies and officials generally. To many clients all these bureaucracies looked the same, impersonal and impenetrable. Some people felt intimidated by what they thought was red tape. They thought the rewards for persisting with enquiries about entitlements would not be worth the effort. This referred in particular to the system for awarding contributory and non-contributory financial benefits, and the tendency among some clients to associate social work with these functions.

Clients' and others' concern with assessing blame and responsibility affected access to services perhaps more than their imprecise knowledge or confusion about agency functions. This concern was a dominant theme when people spoke of their beliefs about welfare, some experiences of securing social-security benefits and their reactions to the moralizing attitudes of relatives. This theme was always present but sometimes camouflaged. Moralizing is often veiled, as between relatives. It would almost always be invisible to outsiders. It is implicit in agency functioning, never an explicit policy.

Clients' accounts of their encounters with officials have the appearance of a clash between life styles. They mirrored some consequences of class divisions. People saw relationships between themselves and welfare organizations as stratified through levels of entitlements and privileges, from unworthy deviants, to responsible citizens to the usually invisible officials thought to control rules and resources. Class consciousness had shaped people's beliefs about the operation of welfare and some experiences of meetings with people in positions of authority had reinforced patterns of behaviour. Orientations to seeking help were not about personality traits but illustrated adaptations to some constraints of economic and social position. Some people had the knowledge and confidence, derived from various forms of social participation, to confront agents and their agencies successfully. Others were very aware that access to services was unequal and that they should struggle to obtain attention and some service. Most clients expected little. Their polite beliefs that everyone had their place, that if benefits existed they'd get to hear of them, were a monument to a system of socialization which welfare-state services had not displaced. Faced with the prospect of presenting their problems to agencies and their representatives, people who had imprecise knowledge and unpleasant previous experience of seeking help from outsiders experienced a sense of confusion and shame. Perhaps 'shame' does not express these individuals' controlling sentiments. Fear may be nearer the mark: fear built from the experience of people who feel powerless, who are powerless; an indictment of a society which prides itself in democracy, which talks of consumer participation and openness in government, which values State responsibility in meeting the needs of its weakest members and which contains helping professions who discuss frequently their altruism.

NOTES

1 Figures relate to two calendar years taken together, figures for the client
   sample relate to information obtained at the time of first interviews. See
   also *Social Trends* 1976.
2 In elaborating their interpretations of the meanings of welfare and
   social work pp. 11–14.
3 All the names of clients in this and the following chapters are fictitious.

Chapter 3

Staff Developing Ideologies

If we could take for granted that social workers always accept at face value what people say they want, and that such staff has the resources to solve problems, there would be little point in discussing some organizational considerations affecting social work. We could assume that social-work agencies were rational organizations geared to respond to the relatively simple variable of public demand. That model of social work is an illusion. People are not always clear about their needs, partly because they are not sure what social workers can do. Staff may be left to guess at a client's expectations of the purpose of meeting. In implementing national social policies and those developed locally by their agencies, social workers have only broad guidelines to follow. Their use of their discretionary powers to interpret people's needs may be influenced by the ideologies of outsiders (Smith and Harris 1972) or by some preoccupation with their agency's public image (Stanton 1970) or by the staff's political motives and their consequent wish to support some disadvantaged people by overlooking certain 'rules'. (Pearson 1973).

Given most social workers' dependence on only a few administrative and legal guidelines and their assumption that resources are almost always in short supply, the practice of social work should be depicted by the notion of caring for only certain categories of people and problems rather than by the more common but uncritical dramatization of this profession's virtues in caring for all. Discrimination between people and problems occurs because of influences and pressures from several sources, such as the values held by members of lay committees or the interest of other professionals whose activities overlap social workers'.

Several conditions facilitate a social worker's management of his job yet pose dilemmas. For example, agency routines provide a worker with a sense of security. But the appropriate response to some individual's urgent need will often involve a social worker in putting himself out in such a way as to disturb his and his agency's well-established work patterns. Other administrators and professionals shape their terms of reference happy in the knowledge that 'inappropriate cases' can be swept under the rug of state responsibility to meet the needs of all its citizens. These other workers – housing or social-security officials, gas or electricity board representatives, police, doctors, lawyers or teachers – may expect social workers to fulfil that responsibility. But social workers are no different from other employees. They also polish certain practices because they are prestigious. They avoid other cases because they are uncertain of the grounds of people's entitlements or of the resources to effect even short-term remedies. In a state of uncertainty they can make only gestures.

In the local authority and voluntary agency only a few social workers discussed their jobs with reference to themselves or how they might meet their own needs through choice of occupation. One said that all her schooling had been completed in a convent and she, therefore, avoided child-care work involving nuns. Another contended that he had spent so many years as a student existing on meagre grants that he identified with people who had financial problems and liked to help them in budgeting and raising money. Most workers were absorbed in knowing about their agency's resources, whether their powers were discretionary or mandatory. They were employed as front-line personnel and had ample opportunity to discuss topics of common interest, swap information, exchange grouses and rehearse treatment plans. They may have forgotten those private expectations of social work which they had held years before when applying for training. They did not refer to them now. Their current reference groups were immediate colleagues, their incentives a sense of controlling work by maintaining routines to achieve efficiency within teams and in collaboration with other agencies. Their sense of professional identity was almost entirely encompassed by the world of work.

This world of work will be discussed in interrelated sections, beginning with information about social workers themselves and the circumstances in which cases were allocated. Staff then talk about ideal goals in each case. In subsequent discussion, however, their definition of cases as 'statutory', as 'crises' or as representing a personal preference, shows their sense of welcoming involvement in only some categories of social work. Their attitudes to the prospect of involvement in certain activities influenced whether any ideals could ever be implemented and show the influence of their assumptions about priorities. These assumptions had been developed before the meetings with new clients and contained the ingredients of several ideologies of practice, not one. These ideologies affected social workers' categorization of clients' needs and their decisions as to which resources were appropriate and available.

The social workers and allocation

'Social workers' refers to full-time employees who were responsible for providing a service to people allocated to their caseloads. Of 38 social workers involved in 60 cases, eight came from the voluntary agency, 30 from the local authority. In terms of experience, low staff turnover, numbers trained and caseload size, these employees experienced more favourable working conditions than colleagues in other parts of Britain (Neill *et al.* 1973; 1976; SWSG 1974). Twenty-one had been social workers before the amalgamation in 1968 of previously separate local-authority agencies. The 17 who had obtained their jobs since that date had an average two and a half years' experience. In contrast to staff shortages in other parts of the country, neither agency had difficulty in keeping trained staff or filling quickly any vacancies. Thirty-four (88 per cent) of the staff were trained.[1]

Caseload size is one indication of social workers' sense of working under pressure.[2] Nine of the 38 felt overloaded with caseloads of over 76. Seven had less than 25 and felt they could visit regularly certain people. The remainder had caseloads between 25 and 75.

Local-authority staff operated in seven area teams, each responsible for tasks in different parts of the city. Team meetings to allocate new cases occurred three times per week. At allocation meetings in the voluntary agency all staff met together and shared responsibility for those who might live anywhere in the city or suburbs.

At these meetings senior staff read out information about requests. Team members volunteered for cases on grounds that they or colleagues thought it was suitable work. An exception to this rule was that out of a sense of altruism provoked during pregnant silences, some staff often volunteered because they felt it was their turn and work should be shared with colleagues.

A general ideology of helping

The planning which led to the reorganization of social work envisaged that staff should implement wide objectives such as the promotion of an individual's full personal development and the strengthening of family and community ties (Scottish Office 1966). To explain social workers' responsibilities, a government circular indicated that they were to promote social welfare by covering all categories of people eligible for advice, guidance or assistance, support or care under any legislation. They were to include those who needed such help in dealing with personal difficulties but who did not come within identifiable categories (SWSG 1968).

Social workers did not dispute the official and utopian terms of reference contained in these documents. In outward communications they shared such ideals because they at least enabled them to take for granted aspects of theirs and their colleagues' purpose and thereby identify a bond between staff who in other respects were different. These shared ideas and ideals constituted these social workers' general ideology (Strauss *et al.* 1964; Geertz 1964).

'Ideology' refers to interconnected sets of ideas which were incorporated in social workers' simplified and convenient interpretations of aspects of their occupation. Several sets of ideas could be identified, beginning with those to which most workers subscribed because they supported their beliefs about the attainment of some ideal state of affairs in the future. This general ideology indicated something of these employees' collective conscience. It was an elaboration of some possible but ideal goals and some means to attain them. These ideals were important, not least because they contrasted with some of the employment conditions which affected their implementation.

Social workers' general ideology manifested beliefs and values which enabled the group to make sense of their work. 'Making sense' involved explaining to themselves and others a reason for choosing their job. It involved adjusting to the implications of the policy that their training and practice should cover an understanding of and some responsibility for almost every conceivable difficulty. It also involved responding to society's dilemma about the value and meaning of help and the desirability of employing professional social workers to provide it. Society's own conflicts about 'help' were reflected in social workers' difficulties in doing their job.

A few workers saw their work as having political implications, as indicated by their welfare-rights activities. Others were involved in special interest groups, such as one for unmarried mothers, and in membership of the local branch of their professional association. But the following description was derived mostly from answers to questions about caseload management.[3] These answers expressed Christian and humanitarian ideals and values. Another key dimension in this occupational ideology was the professional person's use of himself, his altruism and compassion as a means of attaining these ideals.

Following the first interviews with clients, social workers were asked how they would define success in each case. A few had no particular objectives but most referred to practical goals, such as obtaining a facility or further information. Even specific objectives were couched in words about common goals such as 'being happy', 'achieving independence', 'becoming settled'. Success was described mostly in terms of clients' happiness.

> Success would be seeing her happy because if she were happier it would do a tremendous amount for this family.

> To get him into more appropriate surroundings for his physical health which is acceptable to him where he can stay long term and he feels that he is happy and will be able to leave drink alone.

Enabling people to be independent was almost as frequent a goal as achieving happiness. This general objective was used with reference to settling financial problems, helping the disabled to manage better, getting through family crises and even enabling people to terminate their relationship with the social worker.

> The provision of aids enables her to be independent, if not more independent than she has been recently and hopefully if she is now entitled to special grants and allowances we can make sure she gets them.

> I would want to see her more settled but not dependent.

> There are long term and short term successes. Helping her to be as independent as possible . . . but if she can see herself as a person who has rights, who has the ability to use her rights, I think that's progress.

In terms of how success might be achieved, as in references to the value of increasing self-knowledge through establishing relationships, means and ends were sometimes confused. After meetings with a family referred for rent arrears one social worker said,

> We've got to establish relationships with both. And with the young lad in there too. It's not just financial. Probably if we improve the relationship the other side of things would improve too.

Another worker referred to a rootless and lonely ex-prisoner:

> He requires the kind of help that might come from building up the relationship . . . the constant reassurance that you are doing the right thing, the constant reassurance 'No, you are not dependent on me'.

For a few social workers, casework and the making of helpful relationships were synonymous:

> It's casework, helping them to be aware of the difficulties which are between them and looking at why there was a breakdown in communication. Why they might be able to come together and tackle the problems which are there.

Within these sets of ideas specific activities are not easily distinguished from the staff's general reasons for thinking that theirs should be a satisfying job. The ideas expressed those vocational elements in social work – assumptions about the benefits of building relationships – which were not easily translated into concrete and measurable tasks.

It would be difficult if not impossible to hold any worker responsible for not pursuing their client's interests in the manner implied by these ideas. For example, if 'success' referred to a general and uncontroversial state of affairs – such as enabling someone to be independent – no one would know if it had ever been attained or what represented 'failure'. Yet social workers' references to common values and beliefs provided a tenuous link between colleagues and were no more high sounding than the policy statements contained in recent legislation.

This general ideology indicated some consensus. It included some common goals, although my questioning might have led to their ignoring the possibility that widespread economic conditions contributed more to current social problems than the idiosyncrasies of individuals' particular situations. It is probable too that any professional's public affirmation of the purpose of his work will involve some idealistic and unrealistic accounts of what can be done. For example, some social workers' concern to communicate an image of a caring profession inevitably involved them in concealing certain non-caring activities, at least temporarily.

The cost of involvement

Social workers decided each week how much attention to give to those who were already on their caseload. In response to this task they sometimes felt able to implement their general ideology. In other circumstances they refashioned or forgot it. Their attitudes to their work could be discussed under a heading 'How to use your time'. This heading would not highlight the sense of pleasure, mild indifference or even antipathy which staff felt at the prospect of association with certain people and their problems. The notion 'cost of involvement' refers to social workers making assessments of the benefits to themselves in making commitments which they felt they could and wanted to fulfil, or of the 'penalties' of agreeing to be responsible for work in which they were uninterested or inexperienced. Tasks defined as high priorities were expected to be worth doing and usually personally rewarding. Low-priority tasks were expected to incur costs to the worker, if not to the client: a sense of obligation to do something would be accompanied by a sense of only perfunctory interest and anticipation of a later sense of frustration. Past experience had taught social workers that in many cases changes could not be effected easily, that some clients were ungrateful and that time could be better used.

A sense of pressure of time ensured that in day-to-day activities ideals were often forgotten. For example, staff interpretations of agency traditions helped them assess to whom they should respond and how. In the voluntary agency, which specialized in helping single-parent families, the receptionist questioned enquirers about marital status irrespective of any problems. In the local authority agency, former health and welfare officers managed mixed caseloads. Recently-qualified staff took on cases for which their training had not prepared them. All regarded compliance with some agency conditions as an inevitable and often useful routine response to what looked like a baffling problem. As work was allocated and in response to types of cases, they weighed the costs of spending time.

Involvement with some people meant not having time for others. Showing interest in some cases would flatter to deceive because social workers had neither the knowledge or other resources to be able to help. This common and constant preoccupation with the 'cost of involvement' was worked out in different ways.

Some staff planned their week's work but were not always able to fulfil these plans. They, and others, responded in a spur-of-the-moment fashion to 'priorities'. Identification of the latter occurred in informal discussions between colleagues, or as items on the agenda of staff meetings under headings such as 'future policy', 'use of resources'. In this respect discussions resembled round-table boardroom meetings of a commercial firm preoccupied with balance sheets. The social-work deliberations and decisions were not concerned always with spending money. Social workers assessed costs in terms of sensible use of time, of taking on 'appropriate' and 'deserving' cases. Such criteria involved answering questions: how to make the best use of, how not to waste professional skills; whether clients' perceived needs met social workers' priorities; whether crises involved interesting situations in which tangible help could be provided immediately? Sometimes the costs of involvement were considered not worth incurring. Social workers avoided situations in which they anticipated they would feel powerless. In addition, those who presented routine demands in a 'deviant fashion', or who might be defined as having trivial difficulties of little interest, would find it difficult to obtain social workers' immediate attention and/or any future commitment of time.

Local-authority workers assessed costs of involvement by identifying work for which they could easily be held accountable to others. Cases of compulsory supervision with conditions which were binding on professional and client, as in the conditions of probation orders or regarding regular visits to children in care, were tasks of this kind. Such statutory social work was public and visible because it involved the scrutiny of outsiders such as sheriffs, lawyers and members of departmental committees. One area team said they carried out statutory visits for their self-protection. A team member illustrated the point.

> It's maddened me because statutory cases – I think you can ask almost any social worker – statutory cases, that's their priority because there's pressure on you from other bodies. . . . On the other hand, voluntary cases, you are left on your own, nobody is checking on you from here, almost as though nobody is interested.

Those without previous experience of probation were ambivalent about the usefulness of compulsory supervision but admitted that it affected their attitudes towards such cases and to others. Regarding an ex-prisoner not under compulsory supervision, the social worker said,

> I feel that the minute the statutory power is there the client knows it is his own best interest. He has got to be there because otherwise I am going to have to report him. That feeling is always there to a certain extent. I prefer to work without that.

There was consensus among local-authority workers that during each week's work, statutory cases headed any league table of priorities. The responsibility to undertake compulsory supervision was brought easily to mind because there were guidelines to follow, timetables to meet, a performance to be publicly assessed. These expectations gave such cases a compelling quality.

Responses to statutory-type cases showed social workers' assumptions about some agency routines. The cost of involvement was also assessed in terms of the idiosyncrasies of people and their problems as in situations considered to involve crises.

Crises as seen by social workers did not necessarily involve crises as defined by their interviewees. In these social workers' descriptions of crises, several ideas merged. Sometimes they were referring to a particular event, such as cruelty to children. sometimes they were referring to someone's reactions, to that person's sense of loss and grief, their apparent high level of anxiety. Sometimes they referred to a particular situation and to someone's reaction to it. Their comments had in common the implication that defining a situation as a crisis involved a sense of having to act quickly on behalf of someone. They ought to do it. A moral obligation was involved. A senior social worker thought she knew intuitively which people were deserving.

> I think a lot of clients are very demanding and manipulators and you need to watch this. Some of them would have you running every minute of the day and you have to make sure you don't fall into this trap, while others, if they telephone me and said, 'Look, would you come out . . .' There's one woman, I had only seen her once, and I knew there was a real crisis when she phoned and I would go.

Another explained that if the word 'psychiatrist' was used in the referral this heightened his interest.

> I tend to give these cases a relatively high priority . . . here was a girl with a psychiatric history. All the implications were that unless we got a service to her quickly there was a danger of relapse.

The characteristics of someone's predicament were filtered in the light of each practitioner's familiarity with certain resources and remedies. It was possible for members of the public to regard a situation as involving a crisis yet be disregarded because social workers misunderstood or missed certain information, felt powerless to do anything or did not share an individual's point of view. Sometimes other officials influenced decisions. Social workers felt obliged by these others to intervene to prevent situations from getting worse, to ensure that a family were not evicted, that someone regarded as unstable did not break down. In agency terms, 'preventing deterioration' meant avoiding future expenditure of time and money. The local authority's interpretation of Section 12, Subsection 2, of the Social Work (Scotland) Act was that financial help should be given to avoid greater subsequent costs such as those incurred when families broke up and children were taken into care.

Some situations were described as crises when social workers felt they could provide tangible help which would be appreciated.

They enjoyed an opportunity to demonstrate a relationship between their activities and the consequences. Such feedback was important in an occupation in which other professionals were regarded as unlikely to follow up referrals and in which workers seldom knew whether what they did was done well.

These workers sometimes doubted the usefulness of their job. They did not see it as likely to effect change in individual cases let alone on a wider social and political front. In contrast to crises, some work was predictable and routine. 'Routine' referred to *regular* duties such as attendance at courts and at staff meetings, carrying out intake duties, seeing young people who had been asked to report but who 'usually did not say much', making visits to well-known people who were not expected to change or make any sudden, extra demands. Against a background of 'the routine', the recognition of crises was welcomed because it was different and provided reassurances about the usefulness of social work. Some non-routine situations provided opportunities to develop interests and skills. A social worker in his thirties explained,

> I am interested in marital cases. They are cases which I have had for a couple of years and I keep in regular contact. The marital part crops up in crises. It is that sort of situation that I am prepared to spend time on. It's got nothing to do with theories from my training. We had all that Freudian stuff. . . . I resisted it tremendously. The point is when you are called in in marital situations you feel you can do something. I suppose I feel that that's a more appropriate use of my time.

There were different interpretations of appropriate use of time. One social worker wanted to put himself out for certain people. A colleague was less interested in 'that type of work'. In one area team, being available to parents of handicapped children was a priority interest for three colleagues. Another preferred 'the challenge of those with nothing', such as a lonely recidivist just discharged from his most recent short sentence. No other member shared this interest.

In spite of individual differences, preferences for one form of social work compared to another were expressed by general emphasis on training or the lack of it *and* on organizational traditions and constraints. Firstly, likes reflected a sense of confidence derived from experience. Conversely, dislikes were prompted partly by a sense of inexperience. Secondly, some forms of dependency had by tradition been encouraged, others discouraged.

Describing work with prospective adopters, a young social worker acknowledged some relationship between training and employment.

Assessing people for adoption is one of the few areas where you are allowed the luxury of really concentrating your skills on interviews . . . I think this is one of the pure examples of using your training. You are looking for contrary indications to people forming a happy family.

Younger social workers with no more than three years' experience emphasized their interest in 'skills in inter-personal relations'. Older social workers, those transferred from the previous departments, expressed interest in problems with which they were familiar. At allocation meetings they volunteered for cases with particular characteristics such as those involving handicapped children and adults. The statutory social-work responsibility for public burial of the destitute was referred to by an ex-welfare officer.

I do most of the funerals in this area. That's another thing that nobody seems keen to do. Simply because I have done them before I still get them. My colleagues are always saying, 'I'll come with you the next funeral you do', but I am still waiting.

His resigned acceptance that the man with experience should be responsible for making arrangements for public burials underlined also that such work did not match younger colleagues' conception of their role. Regarding other tasks, younger social workers were uninterested because they felt ill prepared, as in work with the mentally and physically handicapped. The same young woman who explained her interest in adoption observed,

Members of health professions may know what they are doing with old people but to us those diseases like osteo and rheumatoid arthritis, I didn't even know there were two types until I met people with different types and wondered what the difference was. It can be confusing if you don't know what a person is suffering from or capable of.

Another, an inexperienced local-authority worker, said,

I'm not experienced in dealing with the mentally handicapped and assessment of places for them. I feel out of my depth in that situation. . . . I have a bit of a block about the mentally handicapped anyway.

The sense of having knowledge and experience affected interests and choice of priorities. Older staff felt secure with previous specialisms. Some younger workers were apprehensive about taking on unfamiliar cases. The social worker who mentioned her lack of experience in work with the mentally handicapped remarked,

I think I have discussed this with several colleagues because I wasn't very happy about the way it was dealt with at the beginning, about the reception we got at that day centre. The mother seems to spoil this child silly. She is an embarrassment to them yet I am lost at just what to say on these occasions. I have to get my colleague's opinion on how people bring up handicapped children.

Feelings about appropriate roles and the value of supporting some clients' dependency were connected most obviously to assumptions about agency traditions and resources. A voluntary-agency worker talked about departmental policy and her interest in one-parent families.

I have an interest in them because I think they have all sorts of problems which we can try to cope with and help in different sorts of ways, apart from the social-work relationship.

A local-authority worker enjoyed her responsibility for a recently separated mother referred for support with financial and other difficulties:

I think it's a case people are interested in. Most people I find are interested in work with families where there are children. Not everybody, but I think it is the type of case I could discuss with my colleagues.

In both agencies, staff were sure they did not wish to risk involvement in certain types of work. Placed in a job in which they felt they had few resources, such as day-care facilities for children, too little guidance about caseload management or too little knowledge of the functions of other agencies, they felt frustrated. This showed in their sense of powerlessness over financial resources and regarding invisible decision-making procedures in supplementary-benefit offices.

At local-authority allocation meetings, if the only advance information about an individual's 'request' was that it seemed to be about financial difficulties, team members were reluctant to volunteer for such work. Voluntary-agency staff also disliked money matters although they had some funds available for their discretionary use. Their agency did not operate under statute and potentially had more control over caseloads, more chance to create its own terms of reference and image. The caseworkers wished to avoid certain tasks but undertook them if they thought they had little alternative. Such practice showed clients' beliefs that 'welfare' was a last resort service to be well founded, although the professionals regarded the functions attributed to them by this public as not their major, let alone a desirable preoccupation. A senior social worker commented,

Personally I just would not like to have too many cases with money in them but because of our interest here in families I think we can't avoid the financial aspect of working with a family.

Dislike of 'financial cases' was prompted by anticipation of being embroiled in people's circumstances with little prospect of predicting events except pessimistically and no prospect of being able to control them. Though several workers were involved in welfare-rights campaigns and talked about the national implications of problems associated with poverty, this seldom made it easy to respond helpfully in individual cases. In both agencies, front line personnel felt confused and frustrated when asked to deal with various material difficulties.

> I hate anything to do with finance. I hate fiddling about with social security and anything like that. I find it terribly kind of, well the thing that really pulls me down and I feel that I'm never really getting anywhere with them. I don't know what's going on down there (the Supplementary Benefits Offices). Even if we go to their office I don't seem to know what's going on. So when I hear about this kind of case I think, 'Oh, for God's sake'. It's not the type of case I want to take on.

Dislike of types of cases was also related to distaste for the manner in which some people were considered to present their request. Those who appeared as though they wanted a quick solution which could involve receiving money were unlikely to be regarded as deserving much time, let alone immediate financial help. At a staff meeting in the local-authority agency no one expressed open disagreement with this point of view.

> I dislike the ones who moan, who are 'hard done by'. You don't mind dealing with someone who accepts reasonably well what has happened to him. If you can help, fair enough; if you can't, fine. I feel that I do dislike people who sort of whine, you know, moan. I hope it doesn't affect the way that I deal with them but you do find that these feelings are there.

Two social workers elaborated their reluctance to intervene. They disliked people who gave an impression of seeking help in an inappropriately assertive way and behaving as though the main responsibility for effecting change was not their own.

> I object to the ones who sort of very aggressively expect you to do something for them and immediately you find you can't. I don't particularly like that kind of person.

> I suppose I dislike people who come constantly for material help. I worked for three years with the RSPCC, so problem families, squalor and dirt don't really bother me. I think I dislike when somebody expects someone to undertake absolutely everything for them . . . you've got to be very careful about this.

Practice-oriented ideologies

My description of the social workers' general ideology of helping was followed, deliberately, with references to their priorities, as expressed in their reactions to the prospect of involvement with certain people and problems. In discussing these reactions they underlined some factors affecting the attainment of ideals. They felt strongly about certain working conditions such as their seniors being interested only in some cases. In relation to some work they showed a real sense of working under pressure. Ideals were not regarded as capable of being fulfilled in each case or by all social workers. The meaning of social work was not only contained in idealized statements of objectives. Social work was interpreted variously. For example, the same social worker defined different aspects of his job in different ways. He held several ideologies. One came close to staff's general ideology of helping. Another was peripheral to it. All reflected aspects of staff training and experience. All were capable of being reinforced by a particular context of work: who happened to be involved in decision-making, what influence they were thought to hold, what advice they wanted to give.

In these workers' management of cases and as expressed in their weighing of the costs of involvement, the characteristics of three practice-oriented ideologies – casework, service, relief – were apparent. Each showed staff making sense of the demands of their job by perceiving appropriate roles, by varying techniques for dealing with problems. These ideologies enabled the staff to make assumptions about how long it might take for some difficulty to be resolved and the extent to which responsibility for obtaining resources should be theirs alone, or might be shared with others, including the client. These ideologies contained the cues influencing staff decisions in particular cases. They were the guides in day-to-day activities.

Casework

In the local-authority and the voluntary agency the staff regarded most of their work as involving intervention with individuals and their families. They reserved the notion casework for an approach which emphasized some understanding of individual psychology and pathology. In each agency the procedures for allocating work to individual social workers' caseloads encouraged any existing trained tendencies to focus on the social and emotional problems of individuals.

A recent national survey of the methods which social work students are taught to practice showed that casework was given most emphasis (Parsloe *et al* 1976). This study's findings implied that casework was regarded as *the* method in social work not just *a* method. Of course, a study of what is taught only helps to explain the world of the educators. The 'fit' between education and practice is acknowledged to be complicated (Stevenson 1977). Yet, casework's popularity with educators and practitioners continues despite lack of evidence about its effectiveness (Fischer 1973), despite criticism that an emphasis on understanding problems in interpersonal relationships is an inappropriate response to nationwide difficulties associated with poverty and unemployment. How can this popularity be explained?

Concepts such as treatment and therapy, which are the stock-in-trade jargon of other helping professions, notably psychiatry, are used frequently to describe caseworkers' activities. The almost mystical reverence given to the importance of 'the casework relationship' can be maintained if it does not depend on empirical evidence of what social workers actually do and if the goals of casework appear sufficiently high minded. For example, in a recent analysis of the claims made by casework theorists, the caseworkers task is summarized 'as [bringing] about an adjustment between the individual and his social situation' although this author adds his own hope that the caseworker's activities may in future be directed more towards society than towards the individual (Ragg 1977). But theories and hopes are not practice. We should enquire whether social workers' assumptions about casework are at the head of any hierarchy of ideas about their occupation. In this respect casework in social work is not being singled out. Such a question requires answers even if critics give a prescription of a supposedly more radical kind. Regarding any professionals we'd still need to know what part of any radical message affected staff's reasoning about their tasks and their performance of them. In addition we should ask if any professionals' taken-for-granted aspirations to do one thing rather than another make it difficult for them either to examine other ways of completing tasks or to pose the more fundamental question about society's purpose in having a particular occupation performed at all. For the time being, however, at least in these two agencies, practising casework was popular with many social workers. They believed that solutions to some individuals' difficulties required different skills than those necessary for the carrying out of 'welfare-type' activities.

The attempt to make distinctions between work involving some practical tasks of 'welfare' and work which focuses on the emotional problems of relationships is one of the major themes in the current debate about 'The Social Work Task' (BASW 1977). Indeed, at the beginning of my research, some senior social workers argued against my taking a heterogeneous sample of clients because this would confront me inevitably with activities which were 'not really social work', as though 'casework' not only took up most of their time but was also central to their image of what their colleagues should be doing. In the past the mystiques of casework relationships may have been accepted by workers with enthusiasm because they defied definition (Timms 1964), but the main issues regarding social workers' current reliance on activities labelled casework can be identified. There are two. Firstly, what are the implications for any one client when a social worker sees his job as involving casework? Secondly, and more importantly, what are the consequences for the personal social services as a whole of selecting one set of activities as being the most prestigious? The blunt answer to this second question derives from the evidence of these social workers' practice-oriented ideologies. Cases which did not appear to require casework intervention merited less serious discussion, less time and other resources.

In the following discussion of these social workers' several ideologies, casework refers to a social worker's art of trying to use his relationship with people whom he assumes to be under stress, in order to mobilize their capacities and resources in their environment to reduce or solve conditions leading to such stress. Casework ideology refers to social workers' assumptions that some work would last several months, would involve meeting people regularly. Given the circumstances of people considered to require casework help, it was assumed that time should, and usually could, be made available.

Casework objectives involved discussing with people their feelings and emotions, their relationships with others as well as with the social worker. The central component of this ideology was the assumption that certain people could and should be helped through the medium of interpersonal relationships. Given this assumption, clients' entitlement to such help was taken for granted. In cases involving other forms of help, more searching questions were asked about entitlement.

The ideas implicit in this ideology were discussed in staff meetings in the voluntary agency which referred to its staff as caseworkers. People regarded as having emotional, relationship difficulties represented these sorts of cases. For example, assumptions were shared about the probable interpersonal nature of an unmarried mother's 'problem': such a case would involve decisions regarding the mother's and child's future; 'one would have to guard against the dangers of making the wrong decision', 'the girl will have to be enabled to think in emotional terms of her baby as a person'. This ideology was central to the general ideology. It reflected organization of resources because it represented work regarded by staff as both a major agency concern and a very important aspect of professional practice. 'Casework cases' provided tasks which social workers were prepared for and enjoyed. Resources were anticipated and could be provided, places in mother-and-baby homes, short or long-term foster mothers, clothes, toys, cots and arrangements to help with payment of fostering fees. Before mothers had made decisions about keeping their child or placing him for adoption they were reassured about available help. In less familiar cases, where well-rehearsed forms of support did not come so easily to mind, social workers were not so able to say what they would or could do in the future.

The attractiveness of people whose problems had looked as though they might benefit from support through casework was illustrated in other ways. They represented the cases which voluntary-agency staff remembered having had as students, as having discussed with supervisors, in student groups, which had provided case-study material for use in staff meetings or in-service training courses. Caseworkers chose to discuss problems which fascinated colleagues, not cases regarded as 'straightforward'.

Service

Some tasks involved collecting information to establish people's eligibility for a facility which could be provided ultimately by others, or regarding a decision in which social workers participated but which they would not make. Such responsibilities involved several meetings with people but could be fulfilled in less time than casework-type jobs. For example, in cases referred to as 'one-off jobs' the beginning and end of giving a 'service' could be marked.

Staff believed that some work could be limited to providing an apparently administrative-type service. Such a term was not used pejoratively. As long as these duties were combined with other tasks, social workers enjoyed service-type work because they assumed it would be relatively straightforward, 'almost like delivering groceries'. Such jobs involved tangible help – providing bath seats, hand rails, telephones, holiday accommodation –

which would not usually require close interpersonal contact and should be limited to meeting the client's or referral agent's request at face value. It would usually not be necessary to pursue other matters.

Typical of cases which reflected the service ideology were those involving old people and the disabled. Inexperienced social workers considered that aged people only required 'something which could probably be carried out by a welfare assistant', a 'straightforward service', such as the provision of aids, assessment of eligibility for day care or more permanent accommodation in old people's homes. It would require no great involvement with the people concerned. Such an assumption had developed because some social workers felt no great sense of optimism about work with old people and others felt lost and out of their depth. Experienced social workers contrasted their attitude to the aged disabled and young people in similar circumstances,

> With younger disabled people there's more that can be done. With the aged it's almost making the best of a bad job, isn't it? I mean we've all got to become old and probably going to be a bit decrepit and in some way or another we've really got to make the best of it.

Another reason for limiting association was that it didn't pay to get too closely involved.

> We don't want over-dependency in the aged because at some stage we have to withdraw. This may be a personal thing but I find it very difficult with elderly people.

Older social workers, who as welfare officers had been able to specialize in work with the aged and the physically handicapped, now felt that such work could no longer be carried out as thoroughly as previously. Carrying a mixed caseload meant giving less attention to the elderly. The importance of this work had been lost sight of in a maze of other responsibilities. A consequence of the unification of previous separate specialisms was the reorganization of priorities. This meant limiting the time available for those who had previously had their own welfare workers. Squeezing out time available for people such as the elderly, because staff felt hard pressed and/or wanted to develop expertise in more prestigious activities, raises the immediate humanitarian controversy over providing an acknowledged lower priority service. In the long term it is likely that the disparity between the number of social workers who are interested and able to work with vulnerable groups such as the elderly and the number in that category needing help will widen. Britain is an ageing country. The proportion of the population over 65 has been increasing more rapidly than other age groups. In England and Wales, in the 15 year period 1960–75, the overall population increased by 7·6 per cent and the population aged 65 + by 28 per cent. In Scotland, over the same period, although the overall population remained almost constant the number over 65 increased by 27 per cent, an average increase of 1·6 per cent per annum and the numbers aged 85 and over increased by 52 per cent, an average increase of 2·8 per cent per annum (*Annual Abstracts of Statistics* 1961, 1966, 1971 and 1976).

Some social workers did volunteer to work with the elderly and disabled because they thought it would involve tasks for which they were suited and which would usually be quick to complete. Whereas in casework-type situations it was assumed that there would be time to work out what they might do, with regard to 'one-off jobs' workers assumed they would either know how to help or they would not, there being little or no middle ground.

Paradoxically, staff from both agencies regarded service-type work as not too demanding and, therefore, an inappropriate task for a person with several years' training. However, contradictions as well as consistencies made up this ideology. Both showed how the social workers coped with categories of people and problems by defining them as short-term, service-type cases, implying that work should be carried out in a certain manner, or, at allocation meetings, avoided altogether. In the context of staff demarcation disputes over appropriate jobs for trained social workers, clients' problems and needs could be easily underestimated or even over-looked altogether.

Relief

Ideas about giving immediate aid were illustrated in comments about disliked cases and situations regarded as crises. The following description is part of an earlier discussion of attitudes to financial problems. An ideology of relief conceptualizes what action social workers considered open to them once they regarded people as having difficulties related to the source and size of their income.

Faced with 'relief-type problems' social workers' first, main and often their only task was to decide questions of eligibility. Regarding material aid, such eligibility was seldom taken for granted. Assessing entitlement to 'relief' involved the social worker asking himself what would happen if he took certain action or what would happen if he did not, what were agency conditions for giving aid and who had to be consulted. Senior staff always had to be consulted if clients were to be loaned money.

Regarding rent arrears and other financial difficulties, referral agent or client would have to prove why their request was a priority. In other parts of Britain and the United States, and irrespective of the extent of poverty in any one locality, social workers have also been encouraged to think that providing financial assistance is a responsibility which they should pass back to other agencies (see Jordan and Moore 1976).[4] In the local-authority and the voluntary agency, each social worker expected that before consulting senior colleagues about giving relief, he should explore every alternative to an individual client being financially dependent on his department. This involved asking people whether they had sought the help of relatives, friends or the Ministry of Social Security. By contrast, problems defined as likely to involve casework implied that a social worker expected to provide at least some initial support, even though the people concerned might not have anticipated or asked for it.

Staff resented being asked to relieve potential crises which had been engineered by the policy of other agencies, as when the Housing Department threatened to evict families. To resolve this dilemma social workers tried to ensure their action could be seen by themselves and colleagues as appropriate work. A decision to give financial help should be made ideologically palatable. It was assumed to be not merely an administrative job but would require skill and perhaps some of the characteristics of crisis intervention. The local authority's policy was outlined by the deputy director:

> The policy regarding the giving of financial aid was to be a casework decision left basically to the practice of social workers on the ground and to their team leaders. The decision to pay or not to pay was to be a casework decision but of course we didn't define what that was.

A social worker caught the flavour of this aspect of policy:

> Casework can be backed up by financial help providing this is watched and providing the department is not seen as somewhere they can get handouts.

Staff felt that they should take particular care in assessing material difficulties because they were running the risk of being manipulated if not deceived. Relief could be given on the understanding that it was not a handout and that contact between social worker and client should extend beyond the immediate difficulty, hopefully until a loan had been repaid or the purpose of meetings had been redefined to include consideration of other problems.

The operational philosophies deriving from this ideology of relief provided as many if not more guidelines about why help should *not* be given, as they provided clues as to whom it should be given and how. By contrast a casework ideology implied that 'help' should be given if possible, although the process of deciding what this help involved and whether the parties shared assumptions about its purpose, was seldom clear. Regarding the ideology of relief, it may look to the outsider who is uninitiated in the ways of professional social work, that unless someone's material problems could be dressed up in fancy language, their chances of receiving financial relief from a social worker were low.

Summary

Social workers' anticipation of the character of different kinds of work reflected some assumptions contained in several ideologies. These ideologies were generated through association with colleagues and in response to several dimensions of practice. These dimensions included technical factors such as some lack of resources; agency traditions, as in a specialization in work with single-parent families; educational influences as in the wish to concentrate on activities which matched some desired professional image. Running through all these considerations and underpinning each ideology were staff's use of value judgements as in their assumptions about the worthiness of certain kinds of work.

The concept of casework is of central importance in understanding these social workers' world. Their ideology of casework meant that if people were thought to be experiencing difficulties in personal relationships, the social worker's role would not be dissimilar from that of any other therapist. This was prestigious social work. By contrast, an ideology of relief implied avoidance of close involvement with clients wanting material help, unless their problems could be redefined. Such redefinition would enable the social worker to change his objectives. Having changed his objectives, the meaning of social work changed too. An ideology of service meant getting involved in tasks which were regarded as not too difficult to complete but which were not seen by every social worker as the best use of their time.

The provision of help by social workers would depend mostly on fitting clients' needs into categories provided by these ideologies. For example, unless powerless people, such as the aged and people living in poverty, could influence social workers into interpreting their difficulties within some plan for casework, they would remain at the bottom of these workers' league table of priorities. These ideologies gave staff some sense of control in a job which confronted them with a range of often baffling problems and numerous opportunities for ingenuity. The wide terms of reference of the Social Work (Scotland) Act have been regarded as giving social workers the chance to use discretionary powers in some novel ways (Carmichael 1969, 1977). But staff from both agencies were concerned to parcel their responsibilities in ways which conformed to familiar routines and some traditional professional ideals. The meanings of social work to these social workers derived from their ideologies and did not always match the spirit of national policies.

In spite of their emphasis on some ideal goals, these social workers felt reluctant to be involved with some people and problems yet welcomed the prospect of working with others. Staff beliefs that some kinds of social work were more worthy than others were likely to interfere with the job of uncovering the problems of the client population.

NOTES

1 They had received a professional award from some College or University or, in two cases, a Central Training Council Certificate in recognition of proven experience, albeit without formal training.
2 Neill *et al.* (1976). In their comparison of social workers' perceptions in four area offices in 1972 and 1975, the authors say, 'Although, for obvious reasons, fieldworkers with large caseloads tended to feel under greater pressure, comments showed that the experience of "pressure" was related not only to the amount of work but also to the social worker's perception of whether work was worthwhile and appropriate.'
3 Questions such as, 'What are your objectives in your work with this family?' 'What previous experience do you have in dealing with problems of this kind?' 'What would you regard as "success" in this case?'
4 They argue that '[social work] intervention on grounds of financial need has been shown both in this country and in the United States to be the least likely kind of referral to lead to sensitive sympathetic consideration of the special problems of such groups. On the contrary it tends instead to debase social work to the level of a particularly odious low-grade public assistance of precisely the kind which was supposedly abolished in 1948', p. 747.

Chapter 4

Face to Face: Assessing and Being Assessed

Were the clients helped by their social workers or not? This is the question which I will discuss in this chapter. But first we need to ask, helped according to whose criteria, the client's or the social worker's? I have used clients' assessments as to whether they had received some service which had helped them. They were asked this question usually at the end of six months.

We can divide the clients' versions of what had happened over six months into two categories, 'helped' and 'not helped'. We should be careful as to what the clients meant by these assessments. Saying that they *had* received help did not necessarily include the verdict that the social worker was a helpful person. Saying that they had *not* received help was not always the same as saying that as a person the social worker was not helpful. For example, an old lady wanted alternative accommodation. A social worker agreed initially to help her towards this end but did not see this person again and acknowledged subsequently that he had overlooked her case. The case has been categorized 'not helped' even though the old lady regarded the social worker as pleasant to meet, a 'helpful person'. Similarly, these positive or negative outcomes did not always correspond to clients' feelings of satisfaction or dissatisfaction. The old lady mentioned above was not dissatisfied even though 'nothing has really happened'.

Ideologies and types of case management

The management of cases depended on social workers' ideologies and resulted in different activities for social workers and different experiences of social work for clients. Therefore, if I was to distinguish only between helped and not-helped groups, I would be jumbling together experiences which otherwise had little in common. For example, two individuals with apparently the same problem each felt helped but their relationships with their respective social workers differed. One unmarried mother was involved in interviews about the future of her baby and from both her and the worker's point of view, the purpose of their association was limited to such discussions. Another unmarried mother became involved with her social worker on a long-term basis regarding problems which emerged as the relationship developed and the purposes of intervention were redefined.

Social workers' ideologies were not mutually exclusive. They produced a continuum of three types of case management ranging from a mixture of relief and service-type tasks at one end to casework activities at the other (Table 4.1). These types of case management can be distinguished by social workers' assumptions about central features of each case: the nature of the problem; the service required; whose responsibility it was to obtain resources; the arrangements to meet (Table 4.1).

The management of 28 cases which were influenced by ideologies concerning service and relief resulted in 12 and 16 in the 'helped' and 'not helped' groups respectively. Of 14 cases in the category showing evidence of service and casework tasks, 11 felt helped, 3 not. Of 17 in the final category, longer-term casework, 10 felt helped, 7 not.[1] (Table 4.2).

Case studies will be used to enable clients and social workers to present their versions of what occurred in their meetings in their own words. I shall give at least two case studies from each type of case management. The first example in each category will illustrate social work in which clients said they had been helped. The second will concern clients who said they had not been helped. After each case study, in order to identify common processes in social workers' case management and some common responses from clients, I will also refer to other examples.

In some cases client and social worker defined help in a similar way when they first met and continued to do so throughout their association. Other case studies illustrate changes, from shared definitions at one stage to different definitions at another. Sometimes such changes led to some service, sometimes not.

Relief and service activities: 'You either get it or you don't'

Helped
Social workers' assumptions that some cases could be managed in a relatively uncomplicated way were typified by a client's comment, 'You either get it or you don't.' Typical negotiations involved in

Central features	A. Relief and service ideologies	B. Service and casework ideologies	C. Casework ideology
Problem	Apparently simple to define. Only one 'problem' or tacit agreement that no more problems require attention	Some familiar features which make social worker collect detailed information	Open to several interpretations. Involves some kind of personal dependency
Service required	Technical service provision or brief assessment and support surrounding recent change in circumstances	Concerns some facility and who obtains it. Meetings leading to 'important' decisions affecting client and others	Involves personal support, clients' needs and help-seeker/help-giver relationship assumed likely to change
Resources	Social worker takes initiative because he has access to knowledge and other resources	Social worker has access to information and other resources but client's resourcefulness considered significant	Individual's isolation from relatives prompts social worker and/or obliges client to maintain liaison with one another
Arrangements to meet	Apparently straightforward. Relatively easy for the social worker to explain	Some clarification of the respective roles is made through arranging appointments	As help required changes over time so too does the frequency of meetings and each party's role
	No. of cases: 28 Mean no. of contacts in 4 month period 2·4 Range of contacts 1 to 7 Most frequent no. of contacts 2 *Examples:* Accommodation and financial difficulties, aids for disabled, applications for nursery school, holiday home, old people's home	*No. of cases:* 14 Mean no. of contacts in 4 month period 5·2 Range of contacts 1 to 10 Most frequent no. of contacts 4 *Examples:* Day-care facilities for handicapped children and for aged, adoption and legal advice regarding custody of children, and placement of children for adoption	*No. of cases:* 17 Mean no. of contacts in 4 month period 9·0 Range of contacts 3 to 25 Most frequent no. of contacts 8 *Examples:* Family support, decisions regarding custody and control of children. Support for single-parent families and single people with combined accommodation, health/financial and related difficulties

Table 4.2   Ideologies and outcomes

Outcomes	Ideologies and types of case management		
	A. Relief and service: short term	B. Service and casework: middle range	C. Casework: long term
Helped	12	11	10
Not helped	16	3	7

such case management occurred in the case of a woman of 40 whose expectations of help were met. She had referred herself and explained why.

> I needed a break away from looking after father. He's 85, disabled, a sort of semi-invalid. For everybody's sake I need a break because I can't go on. He's been in the geriatric hospital and he didn't want to go back. We've explained to father that we all need a break and he's quite willing to go away for a fortnight at least. He didn't want to go into the geriatric hospital because he cried when he was in there. So when I saw the welfare we realized he didn't have to be at the hospital, it could be one of the homes.

The social worker's interpretations were the same. She thought this person was entitled to help.

> Mrs Rose, she seems to know the ropes. She said she's willing to keep her father-in-law. They are happy having him in the family because he's no bother. I felt this request was for the good of the whole family. I don't feel Mrs Rose resents having to care for her father-in-law.

The social worker recognized other problems but didn't feel they merited much attention.

> She [Mrs Rose] mentioned that the family is going through a bit of a crisis, the oldest son's wife is in the clinic. We discussed her family and she told me about the problem they were having with the daughter-in-law but the family is very much one who will cope with these situations and I didn't feel there was anything else. I discussed the family income supplement because she has a big family but they manage.[2] If they did apply she might get 25p more but they just didn't want to bother about that.

The social worker obtained temporary holiday accommodation in an old people's home for the 85-year-old father. She commented on the family's resources and their part in the proceedings.

> It's unusual. They came knowing exactly what they wanted. It was just a formality as far as they were concerned, of putting their name in and having it arranged. I accepted the objective as providing the

service they asked for which was also the service I thought they
needed. When I saw them I didn't feel there was anything else so I
went ahead and made arrangements so that they got this help.

She was involved in meetings with the matron in the home and
with the principal social worker responsible for residential care.

We managed to get a place with no stairs, it's a nice home. I've told
her which month was available and she was happy about that. She
was unusual this woman, she had a clearer idea than some people
about what social workers can do. I felt she was capable and it was a
nice atmosphere. It was a happy home to go into. I enjoyed that.

In this and 11 other cases with similar outcomes, social workers
accepted the problems presented at referral and subsequent
discussion was not cluttered by other topics. Information was
obtained, confirmed and other ideas discarded as not relevant.
Such processes were separate yet linked, concurrent but
intertwined. Each contained obstacles which were surmounted in
such a way that help followed. The first obstacle concerned
information from the referral agent, the second the client's
presentation of their request, the third the worker's access to
resources.

The social workers' selection and retention of information
about the clients and their needs was influenced by their appraisal
of the source of referral. They accepted the client's definition of
the situation, few doubts being shown about the applicant's
entitlement to their time or resources, such as aids for the disabled
or a nursery-school place for the children of single parents. What
they saw in the clients, in their homes, or heard during elaboration
of their requests confirmed what they had assumed at allocation.
For example, a woman asked by telephone for a place in an old
people's home for her mother-in-law on the basis that the latter
had a history of mental illness and now could not manage alone.
The worker therefore suspected this would be more than a request
for registration for a future vacancy. He visited the old lady just
once, judged that she was helpless, that the situation represented a
crisis. Although feeling there was little else he could do (the
daughter was already in touch with her doctor) he impressed on a
senior colleague responsible for residential care that this application was in the very urgent category requiring admission at
the first opportunity.

I've put this application through to Mr Bevin and marked it as being
'very urgent'. He hasn't put it in his 'urgent' file, he has kept it on his
desk. Now that means when a vacancy occurs in an old people's
home he looks through these applications on his desk.

This worker's information that the old lady had been hospitalized in the past and his appraisal of her current state, 'lonely but uncomplaining', living in a 'bedroom like a prison', made him feel that the source of referral had underestimated the situation, the problem was more serious than she had implied. In other cases clients confirmed the information from sources of referral and thus influenced each worker's objectives. Some people limited discussion to the topic about which they believed the social worker the appropriate person to see, because they associated 'social work' with difficulties of only one kind, usually their own.

With the exception of the old woman regarded as completely dependent on others, the clients were seen by social workers as having their own resources such as 'capability in running a home', savings, some guaranteed income, the interest and support of relatives. This enabled staff to avoid pursuing other lines of enquiry and reassure themselves that their responsibility had a fixed end point. In these circumstances, as in principles related to short-term work (Reid and Epstein 1972) a high value was placed on giving each client what he asked for.

In terms of the service required and their role in providing it, social workers responded in two ways. In some cases appropriate resources were available. In others they explained that some facility would be forthcoming, some promise of improvement could be fulfilled but not immediately. Workers were instrumental in getting physical aids and a telephone installed, they obtained a nursery-school place, and temporary holiday accommodation for an aged parent. People enquiring about financial and housing entitlements did not have high expectations but described themselves as reassured that the worker was interested, had done what he could to clarify their position and/or obtain other assistance. In two cases social workers acted as brokers between the Housing Department and a woman living in condemned property, between the Department of Health and Social Security, charitable organizations and a couple whose income had dropped because of the middle-aged husband's sudden disablement. This man described the purpose and outcome of two meetings.

> The price of keeping warm is the main worry. We had no idea what we were entitled to. We didn't know if we should apply for a rent rebate or social security. . . . He's been a help to us because what he didn't know he always found out.

In these cases there was limited personal involvement between client and social worker, little evidence of much negotiation let alone renegotiation about problems. The 'ability to get on with one another' was only a limited feature of these exchanges, apparently not a significant condition of helping and being helped. Social workers' actions matched aspects of their service ideology: the task would be relatively simple, resources could be defined easily and decisions about availability answered quickly, help would involve little more than providing resources such as aids, accommodation or information. There were no shared tasks and few things about which there needed to be consensus (Hansen 1969). The social worker acted, had access to resources and made arrangements to meet the client again or relevant others.

Not helped

Other individuals dealt with briefly felt 'not helped'. They had not received any immediate commitment of time and the assistance which might have followed. Their requests were sometimes accepted yet they were asked to compromise, turned away yet consoled, that common process in personal service organizations of being 'cooled out' (Clarke 1960; Goffman 1952; Adams and McDonald 1968). Such exchanges and experiences occurred in the following case.

A 68 year-old widower, Mr Zebedee, lived in a basement flat. He had not paid several electricity bills and his power had been cut off. He was angry yet tolerated his circumstances until a district nurse, asked by a doctor to visit to dress ulcers on his leg, suggested that he should tell his story to a voluntary organization, the Samaritans. They referred him to the local authority.

On several days each week Mr Zebedee usually spent some time talking with other men who smoked and mused and shared one another's company as they avoided the fresh pigeon droppings on seats in the square overlooked by the voluntary agency's offices. He didn't know for sure what 'the town' did but had heard that they could pay bills. He regarded his request as straightforward. He did not refer to money as such. He wanted help regarding his lack of electric power. He explained why he went to the Social Work Department and what happened.

> I went down there expecting that I'd get perhaps a loan because I'd certainly pay it back. They thought I was well off because I've got that colour TV. My sister died and left that to me, that's how I got it. Watching sport that's my real pleasure but now I can't even do that.

He described the social worker's visit to his home.

> He just nosed around in here, took particulars, just like the police did when they came to see who done the meter. I went to see the Good Samaritans as well, they didn't have anything. It's not right, the winers go and spend their money on anything . . . the man from

the Town House said he couldn't help except he did say if we was in trouble again to go back.

The social worker described two meetings with Mr Zebedee. The first took place in his office a few days after he'd been allocated the case and had invited Mr Zebedee to visit him, the second in the man's home.

> I suggested to Mr Zebedee that I didn't really know whether we could make a straight loan since it didn't appear that he needed social-work help or casework. At the time his main needs seemed to be to have that colour TV switched on. He has a lodger and it's the lodger's need too . . . of course the police had visited and they thought the meter was an internal job. I didn't see that casework was necessary in terms of himself apart from his inadequate money and that was the end of it. On reflection I think he needed a loan but he wasn't well enough off to pay it back.

In the first research interview the social worker gave reasons for deciding that Mr Zebedee was ineligible. Under what circumstances would he have helped?

> I think the main thing would have been his disability and whether he required any aids or finances towards that end. I told him if there was any need arising in the future and he felt we could help and it wasn't based on just a straight gift of money we could look at his needs again at that time.

Mr Zebedee was apparently unaware that obtaining help would require proof of eligibility as in readiness to discuss or even bemoan himself and his circumstances, to relate his general disposition to the ulcers on his leg, his marginal financial position and lack of electric power. Instead he said, 'I need a loan', and so appeared to demonstrate that he wasn't so badly off that his entitlement was obvious. Although he suspected that others probably received help whereas he had been turned down, he accepted the outcome phlegmatically. Six months later his circumstances had not changed. He had had no further meeting with the social worker.

In this case, as in others, a casework ideology interfered with the provision of any service. If Mr Zebedee had been able to dress up his problem in casework terms, the social worker would have felt justified in continuing to visit, perhaps with a view to giving some direct financial help. As it was, Mr Zebedee was unable to present himself and his circumstances as likely to involve a worthy, priority task for a social worker. He did not give an impression that he would participate in achieving any long-term casework goals. Events in this case were repeated, with some variations in detail, in another eight. From an observer's point of view, either party might have focused on different topics than those which led to a request being deflected or dismissed. In retrospect social workers' moulding of information made their case management appear inevitable.

Other unsuccessful short-term cases
The clients spoke of their beliefs about each agency's task to provide quick relief for people who would not have met a social worker unless they had been suffering unusual or extreme hardship. Yet other difficulties might have been included in their stories and been related to their mention of help with specific items, clothes, food, furniture, cash, alternative accommodation. According to our records they could have stressed ill health (three cases), accommodation problems (three cases) and legal difficulties regarding the custody of a child in another. For example, a pensioner couple living in attic rooms were in poor health. The old lady had neither mentioned this to the social worker nor been questioned about it, although she was breathless on climbing her own stairs and contended that she had been even more distressed on climbing those to the agency offices.

The referral agents had 'pushed' people towards these agencies but had provided neither receptionists nor intake workers with messages containing fuller or more favourable information about each applicant. At first glance the sources of referral were not obviously so different from those involved with people who had been helped. In this second group of cases, however, the social workers did not derive either a precise picture of the resource required or an impression of these individuals as deserving. On the contrary, their awareness of people's sources of information about the agency influenced both their interpretations of the seriousness of problems and their view of people's motivation in seeking help. For example, an old lady who saw the voluntary agency's sign from the top of a double-decker bus, who 'thought they might help', was regarded as not seriously expecting help, or as not appearing as serious as if she or someone with more leverage had made the referral, perhaps by letter, thus showing that planning and deliberation had gone into it.

By giving only brief explanations to social workers, people increased the likelihood of their difficulties being under-estimated. They did not elaborate because they assumed the person interviewing them would understand. Their anxiety over some new experience and feelings of shame about financial dependency perhaps explain their conduct and why their requests were seen by social workers as half-hearted, not especially relevant to the agency. These people were likely to be perceived as at best hardly a priority, at worst as trying to get something for nothing, either judgement involving inferences about moral worthiness. In only one case was a second visit made, in only two did social workers visit the client at home, either of which actions could have provided information to change or confirm initial impressions. With limited knowledge, the professionals decided that needs could not be met on that occasion but might be met elsewhere. An old lady with housing problems was advised to visit her councillor, a widow to contact relatives, others were manoeuvred towards Supplementary Benefits offices.

Some staff amplified possible future objectives if people were to return. In this respect they attached more significance to this first meeting than did interviewees. One social worker described her objectives concerning the woman referred by a solicitor.

> There are two main problems. Her anxiety at being left by her husband and her relationship with her daughter. . . . She needs guidance in contacting social security or [regarding] anything else she needs for the house. I see my objective to get her re-established in the community as a person in her own right as opposed to just being with her husband. More might come to light as I get to know her.

This woman was unaware of such plans. The brief interview and the advice to go elsewhere provided little incentive to accept an invitation to return. She commented, 'She was just like my doctor, out the door in five minutes. She was just a young girl, what could she ever do?'

Clients had low or unclear expectations of help and feelings of powerlessness which were confirmed because they saw the social worker as unwilling to help and probably powerless to do so. For example, a man who had been allocated to a social worker at the voluntary agency but then advised to visit the Supplementary Benefits offices, commented.

> She didn't take much interest. I thought a social worker should. . . .
> Of course, it was about half-past two, I don't know if that's her dinner time but she wanted us out of that door awful quick. She didn't ask us any questions or nothing. I did the speaking and she said to go to the Social Security.

Common processes contributed to the termination of each case. These were the underestimation of clients' difficulties and their almost entirely passive acquiescence in being turned away, yet asked to return. Voluntary-agency clients were bemused by such events. They thought the agency existed to help as a last resort, yet they had received only a gesture to match suspicions but not their hopes. One individual regarded such experiences as similar to engaging in a war of attrition, advances only being made after several encounters. He was referring to clothes and furniture, not money.

I've heard people just going down, like us – men not working and then going down and they get the stuff no bother at all. Of course, they've been there before. Seemingly, once you've been there you are all right, your name's down on the books. . . .

Some clients were recalled as not having had much to say, hardly suggesting that they were adept at impression-management, or calculating in their orientation (Levinson 1964; Mayer and Timms 1969). On the contrary, they had shown themselves passive in orientation and in meeting a social worker were unable to influence decisions in their favour. They had presented requests which they thought matched the agency's function and which revealed little of themselves, or which showed their circumstances in the least contaminating light. Deserted wives and the recently widowed who were in arrears with rent and feared the Council, made approaches which to them brought least inference of shame, often mentioning clothes, shoes, food, seldom cash. Their experiences were analogous to the patient who suspects a more serious condition but complains only about a common cold. A doctor gives summary attention and advice that if that prescription does not work to come again. Yet there was little in this first visit to encourage a second, in particular if the client's image of the social worker was blurred and his impression from others was that 'you either get help or you don't'.

Five of these people were retired. None showed the characteristics of the more optimistic approach to seeking help described earlier. To have been circumspect in orientation suggests that they might have had a 'larger repertoire of persuasive appeals' (McKinlay 1974) encouraging the worker to define differently their circumstances and his task. On the contrary, they facilitated his efforts to disengage. Used to abruptness from officials in the past, some were happy with civility in the present, no matter how brief the interview. They did not return, though a few wondered if someone might call to investigate their circumstances, in particular if they had remained the same or worsened. Six months later, sick old people remained sick. People with accommodation difficulties had not moved. Isolated old people still seemed lonely. Tense relationships between two generations were not relieved.

Other individuals' few meetings also resulted in little change in their circumstances but in their experiences the outcome was not determined so immediately. For a time clients shared the worker's interest and optimism. At no point was any clear-cut outcome 'no help' ever 'decided' by one party and realized by the other. Rather, each became involved in enquiries which petered out, leaving relationships which never materalized. The fortunes and fate of Mr Hay illustrate such developments.

Forty-nine year old Mr Hay lived with his wife and nine-year-old son in a three-bedroomed terraced house. Without his knowledge the Housing Department had referred him to the local authority agency because of rent arrears and suspicion of other difficulties. Nine months earlier Mr Hay had lost his job following an accident at work and subsequent medical diagnosis that he was suffering from a form of epilepsy.

Although in financial difficulty, Mr Hay had not wanted to seek help. When feeling overburdened his wife cried and he became angry. He regarded 'welfare' as fit only for the undeserving, the down-and-outs. However, on first meeting a social worker in their own home they reached understanding about an immediate difficulty and possible remedies. The social worker described this visit.

> I went initially just to meet Mr and Mrs Hay. The presenting problem was financial. It was referred by the Housing Department for rent arrears and for help with budgeting. Their debts were about £300.

He spent three hours in the family's home and allowed conversation to 'develop naturally'.

> It's a prevention case. It was presented as financial but a lot of other things have been exposed. I think this is long term. There was a total breakdown of communication between husband and wife. This will repeat itself unless we remain active for some time, until a lot of other difficulties are resolved.

'Other difficulties' included the father's ill-health, the mother's complaints about her angina and hypertension, the vulnerability of the nine-year-old son and a marital relationship which, according to the social worker, 'had not been right for years'. The worker had several implicit objectives, although his immediate concerns were the debts. Following his visit he had kept Mr Hay's army discharge papers with a view to contacting the SSAFA (a Services charity), to see whether financial help would be forthcoming from them. In spite of other work he would find time for this family.

> I've got to provide it, they'll get what they need as far as time goes. They obviously need help and support . . . Mr Hay's discharge from

the army said, 'hard-working, diligent and accurate in all his work,
always well turned out, polite, sober, and trustworthy, popular with
all ranks'.

Mr Hay explained how he had incurred debts since losing his
permanent job and why he did not visit a social worker sooner.

A person that has worked hard all his life is not aware of these sorts of
things. To my mind I thought that Nettle Street[3] was the place to go
to. I think that's in the mind of 80 per cent of the rest of the population. I thought social work was for the down-and-outs.

He recalled a recent visit from a Supplementary Benefits officer.

This man looked round my home and said, 'I see no hardship here'.
I thought, if I'd drunk my redundancy money you'd have given us
help soon enough. Because I tried to put my money in the house,
furniture and things, they seemed to think I was well off. I had
another one come. He said, 'Anyway, you were in the forces, weren't
you, why didn't you contact them before contacting us?' [By
contrast] I found Mr N. [the social worker] was a person prepared to
listen to your views instead of just jumping in without giving you a
chance to speak.

Asked about the problem as discussed with the social worker, Mr
Hay replied.

In my opinion it is really based on financial problems. It's not
marriage. If things are going all right she's a completely different
person. We're getting on fine. But the least little thing, like a letter
from firms, then she just changes . . . There's things I don't know
about and she's been getting letters. I knew within my own mind that
things were in arrears.

Mr Hay was asked for his interpretation of the worker's
objectives and whether he minded such a visit.

Apart from the financial side he was trying to see both sides, where
we were going wrong in the marriage. . . . I found myself at ease to
talk with him. People at Nettle Street had a completely different
approach. . . . You've worked all your life and served your country.
The tension built up in me . . . but Mr N. was able to let me speak
about the things I'm speaking about now without cutting in. At
Nettle Street they kept on saying: 'I'm not interested in this, I'm not
interested in that'. They didn't listen, they just interrupted. In the
past we've tried to have as little contact as possible with welfare
workers. We've worked and if we couldn't work we've starved.

The social worker had created a good impression, plus expectations of future meetings associated with financial help. Yet,
apart from one meeting occurring at the end of three months,
there were no further meetings. Solving this puzzle requires fitting
together assumptions about whose responsibility it was to
maintain contact. This involves considering interpretations of
what was involved in helping and being helped. In this case Mr

Hay's dislike of financial dependence and his stress on the value of independence were a strange complement to the worker's references to self-determination and his reluctance to be seen to be encouraging dependence. Taken together this contributed to each party's reluctance to take the initiative. The professional wanted to be neutral, the citizen did not want to appear to be 'begging for charity'.

Four months after his first visit the worker explained:

I've had no more meetings with him. The door was left open for them to come here if that was what they needed. Mrs Hay came once, I think. I left the door open for them both. I felt that if they were really under pressure, if they needed help they would have come here. The fact that they've been able to stay out of the office indicates that they are managing to cope.

It did not indicate this. The husband's physical condition had deteriorated, his blackouts had become as frequent as one or more a week. His wife was still suffering from angina, felt depressed and had been given more pills by her doctor. Mr Hay wandered the streets in frustration over his unemployment, his sickness, the social worker letting him down. When frustration gave way to anger the son received from his father what the mother euphemistically called 'thumpings'. The boy sat at home all summer.

The social worker was interviewed about his handling of the case. He was reminded that he had considered that the boy was vulnerable and that he would look into this. Why had nothing happened?

Because, one, if I start to run there I shall make them dependent which I've no intention of doing. He is a fairly self-sufficient person up to a point and if I start to dabble too far in there he'll become dependent. That's not going to help.

Whatever went on in this first meeting it had created expectations and assumptions which continued long after the interview had finished (see Roth 1962). Mr Hay said:

I mean, I went through everything with Mr N. because as I said to you at the time there, I thought he was a different type of person to ones I'd seen before. I thought he would be doing something when he came back and asked for my discharge papers and took all the particulars that was in the testimonials that I had and he told me the Army had funds for helping people like me. He told me all these things and he was going to deal with it and well, I was left waiting.

During the same period Mr Hay was also involved in trying to obtain employment; with a general practitioner who thought he was work-shy and had asked him to move to another practice; with a specialist concerning his blackouts. He was also in occasional contact with Supplementary Benefit officers and with a lawyer regarding legal aid in a civil dispute with previous employers. These various officials, including the social worker, never met. They acted independently, unaware of the common factor (Mr Hay) in their activities. He summarized some lessons of his experience.

What I've learned is what I've always thought. Decent, respectable people don't get help. That's my answer to that regarding the welfare authorities. From what I can gather and from the talks I've had with numerous people, those who have got help have more or less badgered them continually and go back and fore, constantly go on until they finally give up. But every person is not like that. Every time you've got to go to a department like that you begin to feel degraded. Gradually you've got a section of the community that is actually being degraded by this type of work or whatever you want to call it.

At first glance Mr Hay's experience would appear to have resulted from a misunderstanding about the social worker's objectives and the respective roles of client and social worker in attaining them. This explanation is too simple. For two reasons, in spite of the initial agreement, failure to obtain some service was always possible. Firstly, the social worker's continued sense of obligation depended on the client showing even more willingness to help himself than he had already. Confirmation of this initial favourable impression was delayed. Secondly, Mr Hay was responding to several people in authority, none of whom had welcomed let alone been able to meet his assertion of a need for quick remedies. He was deterred from insisting that the social worker should deliver what he had appeared to promise because the idea of continually making requests to others was a moral affront to someone who was proud of his independence and also valued preserving some vestige of privacy, in particular because 'going public' had proved previously to be a fruitless exercise. His well grounded beliefs about welfare and his well developed orientation to seeking help would have made it difficult for him to adapt to the implications of casework treatment.

Five other people's experiences were comparable to Mr Hay's. By making enquiries beyond first meetings, social workers gave an impression of being interested. Yet, subsequently, they felt reluctant to take further initiatives and withdrew without any explicit agreement. Following first interviews social workers had no clear impression of these individuals' wishes, felt confused about the 'real' problem and consequently considered it premature to decide what they should do. Although first interviews were followed by visits to people in their homes, still no agreement was reached either about any one problem or undertakings for future meetings. The circumstances of referral and those surrounding a worker's job at any one point in time affected communication. For example, a Mrs Strom, aged 71, described herself as wanting guarantees from the 'social worker' that her mentally handicapped son would be cared for when she died. A home help made the referral and had suggested the possible need for an old people's home vacancy. Mrs Strom had other concerns:

> I want to know that Robin is well set. He thinks he would be able to look after himself in a single room. I would prefer if he was in a hostel.

The social worker regarded the old lady (suffering from Parkinson's Disease) as vague but recalled the home help asking about admittance to an old people's home. This occurred at a time when fieldwork and residential staff were feeling that applications for such accommodation were being made as insurance against future problems not as a solution to present ones. Old people were regarded as assuming that the longer their name was on a list the better their chances of being admitted.

Although people such as Mrs Strom described several difficulties, they apparently gave the impression of speculating what each agency had to offer. Staff felt unsure whether such people wanted help with one problem or just someone to listen to a general sense of grievance. They found difficulty in relating to people whom they regarded as having confused expectations of social work and whose objectives in being referred were not obvious. The way in which administrative procedures sometimes compounded someone's difficulty in explaining their request is illustrated in the case of a Mrs Wells. The social worker recalled the inauspicious circumstances of allocation.

> She had been into intake and gone away. She came in again and was seen by another social worker on intake and it was decided that she should be allocated to somebody, so I took her and she told the story. She had already told it once that day so I think I got a second-hand version of it.

In describing why she visited the agency, Mrs Wells included an apparent lifetime of difficulties culminating in a particular incident.

> My husband was drunk and spent all my wages. He gambled. He used to stay out two or three nights a week and came home when he felt like it. I've had this epileptic trouble and been under a doctor for twenty years and was not able to work myself. He just used to come home and hand me anything he wanted. A week last Saturday I got

mad at him. He was down at my daughter's. He had been out since Friday, 10 o'clock and I never saw him all night. I got mad and hit him. He got the police to me and then he gave me an awful hiding, so I just went up and saw that social worker. When I go and see about a job they ask if you are disabled or anything like that. I have to tell them I take these fits and they won't start me.

A sense of working under pressure and having to find time for other tasks contributed to social workers feeling discouraged to continue responsibility for cases in which they felt there was little they could do. They recognized people's general difficulties but no problem as a priority. The referral agent was not concerned to impress that this person should be singled out or to indicate guidelines for the social worker's role. Tentative plans were shelved when clients seemed disoriented in their accounts of what they wanted, thus reminding staff that their time might be better spent. Mrs Wells' social worker, for example, gave her interpretation of a further visit.

I tried to discuss her marital problems but it was almost as though they had never happened. If she had persisted with the disablement resettlement officer she could have got a job but she didn't seem to want to so I didn't press the point. She doesn't see me as anything other than someone to turn to for money which she really didn't get.

She explained the outcome of the case.

I dropped in there briefly a couple of times but after about a month I closed the case and the file is now downstairs and she is just a card in an index. I have seen her once or twice when I passed coming out of her door so I knew she was alive and well. . . . The trouble was she used to ramble on and on. She was dull. . . . It was almost impossible to have a conversation with her.

Social workers had the impression, as in the case of Mrs Wells, that current difficulties had existed for some time and were therefore not unusual. They saw little to encourage them to try to establish common grounds for meeting and in these circumstances clients' blurred image of social work remained. As time passed the social worker was forgotten and the business of defining problems and seeking help began all over again. For example, at the end of six months Mrs Wells was about to appear in court on a shoplifting charge to which she was pleading guilty. She neither connected the social worker with this event, nor saw her as someone with whom she might have discussed the forthcoming court appearance, although the same worker was to be responsible for compiling a social enquiry report.

Service and casework activities: 'It seems obvious, we've done it before'

Helped

Case management characterized by routine procedures for handling certain requests and problems was typified by a social worker's comment, 'It seems obvious, we've done it before'. This assumption included ideas about 'service-type tasks' and 'case work' but referred in particular to familiar procedures for assessing someone's needs, coming to a right decision and obtaining resources to back it up. The following case study concerns a woman of 58 who had been referred by a health visitor via a doctor as being depressed.

Mrs Quailo lived with her 88 year-old mother. The daughter had suffered spells of depressive illness and spent periods in hospital. She described herself as housebound with responsibilities to look after her mother. She had obtained a booklet entitled *Growing Old, What You Need To Know*, and in red crosses had marked paragraphs referring to specific services. Paragraph 20 read:

> The Woman's Voluntary Service runs the hospital car service for anyone unable to go to hospital by bus. Anybody wishing to use this service should apply through the family doctor.

Paragraph 6 said:

> If an old person is unable to continue to live on their own in their own home they can be admitted to a residential home.

Mrs Q. had been to the agency which issued the booklet, had been interviewed and received promises which came to nothing.

Although articulate and keen to discover her entitlements, she had tolerated for years the difficulty of living with her mother even unknown, she alleged, to the psychiatrists who treated her. She was eventually referred to the local authority by a health visitor. The social worker arrived unannounced on her doorstep. Past experiences and current pressures converged to influence each person's expectations of the current situation and the resources to deal with it. Mrs Q. explained:

> Well, I've been with my mother more or less all my life. She was a widow at 47 and I was a widow at 24 with two little children. So we've just worked more or less together all these years and we've never really been parted for one minute. I've been married twice since then. One husband died during the war. I got married two years ago to a foreign fellow but that's neither here nor there. . . .

I've been tied to the house. I've only had one holiday in my life alone without my mother, that was two years ago. On occasions I sit here crying because I can't get away from my mother. I feel her pressing me all around. I've had several breakdowns and been in the clinic several times for electric treatment. Now I love my mother but she's an overpowering personality, she still is. She's the Queen Bee, let's face it. She's an extra-possessive mother but a wonderful person, very kind to me, would give me the world but she won't give me my freedom.

She explained how she happened to meet a social worker.

Through my son taking me to the doctor the day he found me in tears. I said, 'Nick, I think I'm going mad. I can't take it any longer'. The doctor, he's first class but he said there wasn't a chance in Hell of getting her into a home. When the social worker turned up it was a surprise. I'd never met them before, just the depressing one (a reference to health visitors). There's the very depressing one and there's Miss A. She's nice, she really is, but she never does anything.

According to Mrs Q., the first meeting with the social worker was short and didn't promise much. She regarded the age and sex of the social worker as off-putting, although ultimately such an initial reaction was unimportant.

I thought he was very young for the job and didn't actually think he'd get anything done. I'm being perfectly honest, he seemed a bit wary of approaching my mother. He says he's going to do something, I'm very surprised. He says he'll try and see more or less about getting her into a home.

The social worker was concerned which person's needs were paramount and he speculated about other problems.

I'm working with the whole set-up. It was the daughter I interviewed, she's the one with the most problems. There was a presenting problem which was the old lady and her care. The daughter seems to have had some marital tension. She's a nervous sort of person as well. I think she'd had treatment at the clinic and hospital before.

Researcher:

Do you propose to get involved in these other things, the 'marital tension', for example?

Social Worker:

It was initially referred for the old lady. Having gone there Mrs Q. was on about her marriage and the tension and how her mother's presence had aggravated it. The objective becomes providing relief for that particular situation probably via day care in one of the homes. If you take the place of an unqualified psychiatrist you can get into deep water. . . . I think it's still at the stage of making an assessment really.

Several factors had a bearing on the social worker's decision: his prior experience; his interest in the woman because of her psychiatric difficulty; a certain resource was available and needed to be used; the client was regarded to some extent as able to help herself. He decided that day-care for the old lady would be the best way to deal with the daughter's difficulties.

Where I worked before, all the old people's homes had a quota of about six people they took into day care. That department even provided transport and employed a couple of drivers to do this. With Mrs Q. and all the tension in her home the objective became providing relief for that particular situation via day care in one of our homes. . . . In a way their problem fitted in with things in our department. The matrons aren't keen on their homes being used for day care and there's only one or two people going to this particular home. We've only just introduced the day care business and because of [matron's] opposition, I knew that if we didn't use it it would probably lapse. . . . But it was only possible to use that form of help because the family could provide transport.

Subsequently, the family couldn't take the old lady to the day-care centre and the social worker transported her. He explained why:

When they couldn't manage after a few weeks I decided I would take Mrs W. [the mother]. I didn't want the system to lapse. I was a bit concerned because I knew Mrs Q. had been to the psychiatric clinic before and she might be heading for another breakdown. I'm familiar with taking applications for old people's homes. The objective is usually to keep old people at home for as long as possible by providing extra domiciliary care. But this case is far more interesting than the usual ones.

Arrangements to meet were clear to the social worker.

For the next couple of months I'll probably go up once a fortnight to see how things are going. I'm wanting to check to see if things have been alleviated because I think this old lady's presence has created tension. It might be interesting to find out whether day care has been successful, or whether the solution is to admit her to residential accommodation on a permanent basis.

Mrs Q. interpreted the social worker's role:

He's more or less seen about getting her into the home, hasn't he? He's in touch with the matron up there. He sees me regularly, but it's completely different from the health visitor. She just comes in, 'How are you today Mrs, and my, you are looking well, your knitting is beautiful', and so on, and away she goes. Yes, she is very nice but as my old man used to say, 'Stories are no use, it's action that's wanted'. With the health visitor it's just a routine visit. I suppose she's doing her job, she's probably got a rota thing, but he is doing something. I didn't think he would at first but now I think the world should be full of Mr R's. I prefer him to come to the home, you are on your home ground there, you know. . . .

Meeting Mr R. was different from her experiences with others. She was concurrently seeing a general practitioner about her husband's sickness. To her that doctor was vague, uninterested and unwilling to treat her husband for his 'drinking problems'. He brushed her aside.

In other cases social workers also decided that there were procedures to be followed with people and problems worth their attention. According to each party's accounts, these ranged from requests for facilities for handicapped children, to adoption applications, to interviews with women recently widowed. People were involved with social workers in discussions about their or the referral agent's request and possible 'remedies'. In some instances they acknowledged each social worker's assumption not only that interviews were reciprocal exchanges but also that aspects of decision making should be shared. Interpretations of 'problems' and 'help' were influenced by some sense of relationship. People clarified expectations and said what they needed, each worker acknowledging and often appearing merely to follow each individual's wishes. Management of resources was ostensibly mostly the social worker's concern.

In addition to information derived at referral, social workers felt they had fore-knowledge of certain problems such as the care of aged spouses or parents. Experience gave a sense of knowing a stressful situation which might be relieved, of taking for granted that some individuals' needs had implications for other family members. For example, the secretary of a pensioners' club referred one of her members regarding a husband described as ageing, incontinent and frequently violent. A widow was referred by a health visitor as 'requiring support'. Social workers accepted these requests at face value. They confirmed that circumstances were difficult but might be alleviated, in one case by enlisting a doctor's support to admit the old man to a psychiatric hospital, in the other by checking the woman's physical health, living conditions and the links between them. Idiosyncrasies in these social workers' background influenced their interests. One had been responsible for the supervision on probation of another member of the pensioner's family and took for granted that alleged trouble with the father would be genuine. Another had trained as a nurse and was now attached as a social worker to a doctor's surgery and health centre. She was interested in people's physical health and diet, as well as in clarifying their entitlement to financial and other benefits.

Staff reactions that these were interesting requests were influenced by their perception of clients' motivation. Adoption applicants and parents of handicapped children were 'keen to cooperate', 'competent in representing their interests'. Unless clients had other wishes which they did not express, the potential for misunderstanding about their immediate needs was low. For example, doctors and a representative of the local authority Education Department had referred families for consideration for day care for mentally handicapped children. These sources of referral had specified what was required and its importance. On meeting parents the respective social workers' impressions derived from previous information were confirmed. For example, a senior social worker had received the Education Department's written recommendation that a teenage boy and his family would benefit if the boy could attend a day training centre. This senior social worker wrote a memorandum to a colleague,

> They [a senior occupational centre for the mentally handicapped] are very short of places and it will have to be a priority selection . . . it will have to be an individual decision between the family and the social worker.

In another case involving a mentally handicapped child the cues from the source of referral were slightly different. On this occasion the social worker was asked to deal sensitively with the parents. A doctor at a children's hospital had written:

> At four years old he shows a very marked developmental delay so one suspects he is going to be mentally handicapped. Any social work intervention, as I am sure you are aware, would have to be gently handled. The couple are aware of the referral and would be grateful if you would provide the necessary social-work services to the family.

An experienced worker who had specialized in helping families with mentally handicapped children volunteered for each of the two such cases. Having met the parents she felt certain about their needs and her role. In the case of the referral from the children's hospital doctor she suspected the mother had not accepted some implications of the child's condition. Later, after also meeting the father,

> I made out a background report for the nursery and for the assessment team and had some discussion with her. I feel he should have a high priority for attending the nursery a few days a week to relieve the home situation and to give Wayne the benefit of learning from other children.

The same worker described how the other family's story influenced her decision regarding their 16 year-old son.

> With the James family, I realize, even with just having seen the father, that if Donald did not go into a senior centre, the mother is going to have to give up work. This would create resentment and make it difficult for them to cope. It might in the end lead to a breakdown in the family, having him admitted to a subnormality hospital.

This social worker was impressed by the attitude of other family members.

> Usually families say that they need a lot of money but I would say that this is partly escape. It's unusual to find grandparents willing to help out, the extended family giving help and taking their share, so that mother and father can go out. Maybe this is because it is a fishing village [referring to where the grandparents live] and they have a sort of built-in cultural pattern of looking after their own.

The social worker judged these people worthy and anticipated what might happen if they did not receive appropriate support. She forecast difficulties if a place were not found in an occupational therapy centre, almost as though future developments could be mapped. She was following a familiar route. There was 'information' that needed corroboration, such as the family's attitude towards the handicapped young person. This involved discussion with family members and forwarding information to residential staff.

Written and unwritten rules guided management in two kinds of adoption issues. For example, three unmarried mothers and a recently divorced father with older children had been referred to the voluntary agency. Two couples applied to the local authority agency to become adoptive parents. Staff followed their normal procedures. Questions to be explored, such as a couple's attitude to bringing up children as well as their relationship with one another were 'known'. Familiar interview techniques followed the assumption that it was good practice to discuss the information on which decisions about suitability as parents would be based.[4] Although having routine characteristics, such cases were allocated easily because they were regarded as prestigious and likely to be interesting. A worker who interviewed a single woman expecting a baby took for granted the topics to be discussed.

> She is an unmarried mother and she is aged 35 and she is slightly above the normal age we get. . . . She realizes she could be faced with quite a few problems due to the fact that she is a single girl. The objective in this situation is that one has to arrange for a child coming into care once it is born and one has to be prepared for any support that the mother may need in post-confinement when there

could be a lot of other problems especially with whether or not she should allow the child to go forward for adoption.

Assumptions about what to do would remain an academic exercise if the worker could not follow through in future meetings the commitments made in the first one or two. However, anticipating a set of procedures and the topics to be explored gave staff a sense of security about their roles. This contributed to a momentum of interest and a framework ensuring that such requests were unlikely to be misunderstood or overlooked.

Implementing decisions involved not merely a social worker's interest and industry. On the one hand his perception that requests required several interviews was linked to a feeling that he had the knowledge to manage such work; on the other, these people regarded keeping in touch with the social worker as in their own interests, some being unwilling to take 'no' for an answer. From the point of view of those who had imprecise expectations of what a social worker might do, that person's intervention clarified his job and their difficulties. At the end of four months a widow who had received money for a special diet also mentioned her loneliness, at which point the worker introduced her to a volunteer visitor. Intervention in another case resulted in an aged man being placed in the geriatric wing of a psychiatric hospital. His wife had not expected a social worker to be able to speak to a doctor about her husband. People who had expected merely to be assessed regarding their entitlement to some facility, also described the results of a social worker's intervention in other ways. They referred to support by means of the opportunity to express feelings. For example, the grandmother of a mentally handicapped child needing a nursery school place found the worker interested and authoritative, her style encouraged communication.

> I had asked my son's doctor and he gave me a great shock. He said, 'Oh, he'll never earn his own living'. So at this time I was grateful to Miss S. for all her kindness. . . . I was able to talk about it. I didn't mind with her. Somehow there was something that was just there. . . . She's the only person I felt I could open out and talk to. I haven't even discussed it with my husband. I certainly wouldn't go to my own doctor. I couldn't even speak to the boy's doctor all that much.

The father who wanted to place his children for adoption said,

> I didn't know she would deal specifically with this and I didn't realize their scope was so large. She eliminated a lot of fears that I had. My fear was that my boy might think I was giving him up, sort of thing. . . . She's very easy to speak to and understanding all the way

through. With lawyers it's mainly a professional job for them, they don't take a personal interest in it. They wouldn't show any feelings and not really any interest. The social worker didn't behave as though it was a job, even though it was.

A combination of service and casework-type activities in the above cases involved social workers in obtaining day care for mentally handicapped children in nurseries and an occupational centre. In six cases regarding arrangements for adoption, staff enabled mothers to decide whether to keep their child and clarified too the ambivalences in a father's proposal to begin 'a new life' by placing his three children for adoption to his previous wife's new husband. Prospective adoptive parents were eventually passed as suitable, one couple squeezing through on the casting vote of the worker involved. Two mothers stuck to their original intentions to place the babies for adoption and two kept their children. Workers supported these latter decisions because they regarded the mothers as having sufficient resources and resourcefulness to look after their children, at least at that stage.[5]

Not helped
In contrast to short-term work in which staff felt discouraged because they saw few ways of intervening, in other cases (categorized 'middle range') social workers tried to meet clients' initial expectations by, for example, obtaining a vacancy in some appropriate facility. The people concerned rejected the offers. They, rather than the workers, decided that contact should cease.

Social workers volunteered for some new cases because the tasks, such as enquiring whether some facility was available and on what grounds, appeared familiar. Such work also had unfamiliar features whose implications were not immediately clear and staff expected to need more than one or two meetings to get to know people. Such tasks included enquiring about hostels for people discharged from psychiatric hospitals, sheltered housing for old people, nursery and other day-care facilities for mentally handicapped children and adults. At allocation, social workers had thought their tasks would be relatively simple but their assumptions had changed on meeting the families. They were not discouraged from having further meetings. On the contrary they persisted in trying to obtain, firstly, a clearer picture of the family's request and its implications, and secondly, more information about available resources from others – health visitors, housing officials and colleagues. They also took families on visits to the facilities concerned and/or fed back information. They assumed it was their responsibility to nag at a problem and tease out the possibilities of a solution. A worker who felt she should take almost all initiatives regarding aged and disabled people said she did so because these were dependent people and such activity complemented her 'practical frame of mind'.

These clients began knowing what changes they wanted, albeit without considering all the implications. For example, a health visitor attached to a doctor's surgery referred a couple for enquiry into their possible entitlement to sheltered housing. They felt they were becoming frail and their house too large. They and others such as parents of a teenage mentally handicapped child had some experience of meetings with officials. They were aware of being involved in some sort of bargaining. They began with clear if not high expectations of help. The social workers sketched-in information. The interviewees changed a general expectation of what might be possible to a sharpened perception of what was desirable.

Within one month with three meetings, one worker obtained an offer of a place in sheltered housing and discussed with an aged couple how to transfer their accommodation. Others obtained lodgings for a young mother and her child and a place in an occupational therapy centre. In two instances the families were taken to the respective institutions and introduced to staff. The offers were turned down when the would-be applicants changed their minds. The elderly couple felt reassured they could stay in their own home a little longer, yet could move in the future into sheltered housing. Armed with new information they decided that they did not want sheltered housing 'of that kind' at that time. A parent explained her rejection of a place in a day-care centre for mentally handicapped children, even though she realized such vacancies were hard to come by.

> No, I didn't like Regal House at all. I didn't like the woman who ran it. Let's say she was far too strict and not sympathetic or understanding as far as I could see, which wouldn't have done with Joan. I believe in a bit of freedom of expression, even for mentally handicapped people. They are not as stupid as you might think, you know – the mentally handicapped. I don't think it does them any good just to be dictated to all the time, told to do this and not to do that.

Social workers' actions influenced clients' decisions. Applications for hostel or day-centre accommodation began with each party having some sense of understanding that such a facility was required. A by-product of communication about available resources was that decisions which once seemed to involve an obvious if limited solution were reinterpreted as no longer such an attractive choice. People obtained new information and changed their expectations. Such social work involved giving information to enable people to reject one offer and choose an alternative, to feel sufficiently secure to influence the direction and outcome of bargaining, albeit by saying 'no'.

Such rejection was an unusual example of clients' influence but not a surprising outcome of meetings. In the literature about personal service organizations there are few examples of clients directly influencing professionals' practices, of openly rejecting a professional's prescriptions (Stimson 1974). People's ignorance of services and inexperience in negotiations usually place them in a powerless position. However, people, with clear expectations of help have some frame of reference from which to assess not only a social worker's attitude but also the quality of the facilities offered. Such circumspection was a feature of these exchanges but it is an artefact of this research to imply that only those with that orientation to managing relationships with officials would be capable of insisting on change through improvement, yet subsequently reject what was offered because they had reassessed what such change involved.

Casework activities:
'There's more to this than meets the eye . . . almost always'

Helped
This quotation illustrates a worker's assumption that many people would have hidden problems requiring close personal support. 'Support' could be demonstrated through the duration as well as the intensity of relationships between a social worker and a client. For example, in 17 cases, including seven in which people said they had not been helped, there was a mean number of 9·0 meetings between the parties over a four-month period compared to means of 2·4 and 5·2 in other types of case management (Table 4.1). Clients might accept or resist social workers' intervention. Either response was regarded by the staff as confirmation of beliefs about the long-term work required: the clients' acceptance was welcome encouragement, their resistance evidence that their difficulties were akin to the visible portion of an iceberg (see Scott 1969).

In some cases the parties shared continuously their inter-pretations of problems. In others the processes of assessing and being assessed were not so simple. The following case study depicts clashes in perspectives even though, ultimately, views merged and attitudes changed.

The case concerned an unmarried mother-to-be. The girl, Mary, described her predicament and how she eventually met a social worker.

> I didn't want to admit to myself that I was pregnant, I didn't tell my parents. I suspected but I was too scared even to go to a doctor. When I went there (to a hospital out-patient department) they put me up to the ante-natal. . . . When I found out I nearly died. A woman up there, she talked posh and had a long cigarette holder, sent me down to see Miss K. [the intake worker at voluntary agency]. They said I'd have to find out about a home. . . . I suppose money is my biggest problem. I used to be making about £14 a week, now I just get £6 on a maternity benefit book.

After months of apparent anxiety Mary reached the caseworker via a hospital out-patient department, a medical social worker in a maternity hospital, and an intake worker. She liked the latter person but accepted being passed on to someone else. Mary was in unusual circumstances. The route of referral added to her uncertainty.

Mary's situation was not new to the social worker. Her experiences with other unmarried mothers affected her initial attitude. In discussing 'the problem',

> It's obvious she's pregnant . . . not exactly like a financial case which is usually not financial. It's often something else. But these lassies come expecting you to take a moral attitude. She'll have to stay in contact with us because it's a problem that won't go away, her emotional problem about keeping the baby or placing it for adoption. . . . There's a boyfriend involved and I may have to work with him a bit. It's a complex situation, she really needs someone from outside it.

The service required was clear if difficult to express.

> I want to help her make the right decision for her. I can't think of anything more heart-breaking than deciding to part with your baby and then deciding that you want it . . . at the moment we've got to provide her with certain practical facilities, we've got to provide her with accommodation, but basically the most important thing will be interpersonal help.

Mary did not expect this person to continue to be interested once she had a room in the agency's mother-and-baby home. The social worker took for granted there would be value in continuing to meet the girl indefinitely, and began to make weekly visits to Mary.

I'm just trying to get to know the lassie, I'm going up there generally to chat about herself, her ideas about the baby, and then I feel I can go on from there. There's a few administrative things we can do, she's got worries about her insurance and social security. We can tie that up, I'll speak to her about the fostering and the other procedures. I think that's really what she wants at the moment. . . . At the present Mary is pretty set on adoption. If that was so I would see her up until six weeks after the baby is due until she signs the consent, which is a period when she is back to 'normal'. If she keeps her baby we'd go on supporting her, helping her with day-nursery things. It's getting near the time when the baby will be born and it will be useful to see her. . . . One is trying to get closer so that she will come to you with anything that is worrying her. In a way you are trying to get her to look at herself and her emotions, what she's feeling . . .

Having settled in the mother-and-baby home, Mary referred to her family's indifference. She felt isolated and rejected.

I told my boyfriend. He's not really interested. My father's only found out a week ago, he's the worst. I was petrified to tell him. My mother told him and he raved on about how I had ruined my life and no decent bloke would have me. My mother said why don't I get an abortion. He stopped speaking to us for two days and I've got to get out. My mother says it's all my own fault. My father got really mad – 'You'll get out', he said, 'the neighbours will find out, go and get somewhere to stay, you are not staying here'. My parents just thought about the scandal and the shame.

The clash between the girl and the worker centred on Mary's interpretations of the worker's wishes regarding the baby. She explained the events leading to an outburst:

Nobody really seems to care. The doctors at the clinic make me feel guilty about the baby, having it and wanting it adopted. My dad's come here but he's embarrassed. Mum says it would be nice to keep the baby. Most of the girls in here talk about their babies. They usually decide to keep them. Nobody really seems to help you. I was scared stiff of having the baby at first but now I can't wait to have it.

Referring to the social worker's visits:

It's embarrassing when she comes, she just sits and says nothing. She looks a typical social worker with a briefcase and papers. She never asks about anything but adoption. I think she wants me to keep it because she keeps telling me the things which the social does for mothers and their babies but she never really says so. . . . I'm usually talkative but not with her. I think it would please her if I kept the baby because the only thing is she keeps telling me what the social do if I keep the baby and they'd help me with looking after it.

The social worker heard of Mary's feelings from the residential staff.

> I heard from the matron that she was crying and rushing down the stairs saying, 'that bloody woman wants me to keep my child'. I was upset when I heard she had called me everything under the sun. The lassie is pretty muddled, I suppose she had to blow up at somebody. Now I think I had better make more casual sorts of visits.

At this stage the social worker's therapeutic aims were, perhaps inevitably, not understood. Her somewhat non-directive, passive style apparently increased the anxiety of a young woman whose immediate future was very uncertain. However, ten months later this girl's interpretations accorded with the social worker's original appraisal and her feelings had changed. This gradual change was associated with particular events. Following the baby's birth Mary decided to keep the child. The social worker demonstrated her concern by practical help, providing a pram, making temporary arrangements for fostering and agreeing to see Mary's boyfriend who some weeks later became her husband.

Within a year Mary moved through various 'crises', from deciding to keep her child, to returning temporarily to her home, to getting married, to the break-up of her marriage and subsequent fostering of her child when she returned to work. In contrast to Mary's confusion and anger when she was in the mother-and-baby home, she and the social worker had developed similar perspectives and similar feelings towards each other.

Mary's increasing dependence reflected decreasing 'personal resources'. With Mary immobilized partly by uncertainty, only the worker seemed able to act as intermediary, see the parents and meet the husband. After four months the social worker had become a virtually taken-for-granted resource. Mary's perception of the service she 'wanted' incorporated objectives which the social worker wanted to fulfil. A relationship developed, as evidenced by the girl's growing confidence in the social worker's attitude and helpfulness.

> I never had much faith in Mrs S. at the beginning . . . she seemed depressed but now I've got to know her she's a real help. She's got baby-sitting for me so I can go out to work.

A few weeks later Mary explained.

> My husband beat me up and we had a terrible row in the street. I went into a phone box and she came straight out. I've got the feeling that Mrs S. is worried about us and my marriage. She wants us to stay together – she's sympathetic and you know she cares. She's helped with coal to avoid getting too big an electricity bill. You feel you can drop in on her any time, the same as she can drop in here.

The social worker explained who maintained contact:

> Very much a bit of both. When things get too much for her she will

phone me up and I'll go out or she'll come in. If things look as though they are a bit more settled then I'll visit. I used to go in every week although she wasn't requesting this at first. At present (11 months after the case was opened) there's not really a crisis, she's just ticking over. I see her weekly to see how things are going and how she's feeling.

In some ways Mary's dependence met needs in the worker.

I've probably got a lot more out of this case than, say, with old people. I've got to know Mary well and her husband for as much as you can actually get to know him. It's meant a lot to me. It's even kept me awake at night but I've had rewards. I've seen it progressing.

The social worker referred to hers and Mary's initial incompatability, what she had been doing and what she might do in similar situations in the future.

Looking back, what happened at first wasn't surprising. Maybe you've got to force yourself on for a wee bit with these girls so that if anything does happen you hope the lassie will come to you in a crisis and that's what happened. You have to make time with a case like this. I felt it was important when they asked me to go and see them, but with a lot of old people you can afford to put it off till tomorrow.

Mary explained her gradual acceptance of some of the worker's views and how their relationship had developed in consequence.

She's making me see that I've got to stand on my own feet. She told me it would be stupid to try to go back to my husband. Early on I wished she'd said whether or not to keep Alan. Now it's me that's needing to see Mrs S. not her needing to see me. When she first came to see me at the home I thought she was checking up. She kept saying, 'I want to see you next week at such-and-such a time'. Now I know everybody in the agency. The receptionist knows me. She's always sitting there. . . . Mrs S. talks a lot more now. That makes it easier.

Mary had altered her appraisal of the social worker. She liked her for characteristics, such as respecting the confidentiality of personal information, which she had not anticipated and seldom experienced previously.

When I broke from my husband the foster parents didn't know anything about it, even though they must have asked Mrs S. lots of times how I was getting on. I don't suppose I would have minded if she told them I had broke up from Ron. I was pleased when I found she hadn't said anything.

Other examples

Common processes in other long-term work in which people acknowledged being helped concerned workers' initial perception of casework-type problems (Stage One, grounds for intervention);

cementing of understanding in subsequent meetings (Stage Two, confirming eligibility); a final culmination of events depicted by reinterpretations of social work and social workers (Stage Three, conversion to professionals' points of view).

These people were referred apparently because of circumstances associated with their recently changed family and marital status. Three married women with children were referred by their husbands (two cases) and a doctor. A single girl thrown out of her home by her father was referred by friends. A divorced man recently discharged from prison referred himself. A woman recently widowed had been referred by a health visitor as being disabled and depressed. A boy of fourteen who had allegedly been involved in delinquency but not charged, whose mother was disabled, whose father was away from home, was referred by police. Their expectations of help were vague because they knew nothing of the referral or because their beliefs made them feel ashamed at the prospect of meeting a social worker. Indirect routes of referral and their limited participation in it affected their assumptions. The widow said after her first meeting with a social worker,

> She was very nice but I mean, when you've only been in this position for the first time you don't know how they can help. She seemed to be the type of person who could help just talking to you.

Staff considered these people required outside help because they had neither friends nor the support of relatives. Alternatively, they were regarded as experiencing a crisis, as in reactions to a husband's sudden death or desertion, an unusual situation for a family and as such an important test of staff commitment and ability. However, initial exchanges were characterized by staff recognition of serious circumstances rather than explicit agreement about a problem. Seventeen-year-old Diane's worker explained:

> The first time she came in I could see she was so ill, she'd wandered the streets all night. I felt this wasn't one where I could say, 'Well, I must visit your home and see what has happened' before I got her in somewhere because she was going to drop. I'd heard about her problems a bit from other girls. Normally we try and investigate a bit more about the home but she was so ill I felt I had to get her some sort of care.

Diane described some family experiences and why she had not minded being referred.

> I thought things might be confidential there. I get depressed. I've an awful lot of troubles. It was a lot of things mainly from the day I was

born right up to now. I never had a happy life. My mother is always getting battered by my father and he's battered me as well. Five weeks ago he battered me for getting on to my mother. He battered me and threw me out, so I was black and blue from my head to my shoulder, well, from the top of my neck right to the end of the other shoulder. I haven't been back there since.

Difficulties surrounding referral, including ignorance of social work, were nullified by reactions to staff. An individual's wish to see a worker again was affected by his feelings about the worker's attitude or disposition as much as by what was said. Such 'style' affected a client's sense of feeling accepted and at ease. A woman referred by her doctor:

I didn't know social workers had anything to do with doctors. Miss Pryce turned up one day. I didn't know about it. I just had a feeling in me as if she'll speak about anything and everything. It can be about the children, it doesn't have to be about yourself or the house or things like that.

The social worker reciprocated the woman's feelings.

She was interesting, a likeable person. I wanted to help her cope with the difficult situation she was in, to come to terms with it. I recognized it was difficult for her to accept that her husband had left and in some ways she thought she hadn't succeeded.

As in the case of Diane, workers responded to people's wish to speak to someone outside their family and in confidence. Asked why she went to a social-work agency, one young woman replied,

I just wanted to speak to somebody, you know what I mean. You can't speak to your own folk about things. They tell you one thing and you want to do another. If you are speaking to someone you don't know, you calm down a bit.

Understandings achieved in first meetings reflected not so much shared and explicit definitions of problems as some rapport between help-seeker and professional. The latter felt a need to take some action, the former that their difficulties were appreciated. The one was perceived as helpful, the other as needing help, reactions which were confirmed subsequently. As in the case study, even if problems were not defined similarly in first meetings, the social worker confirmed later that someone merited continued support. Such an outcome was enhanced when people's responses implied acceptance of the worker's objectives, as when parents recognized one worker's concern to examine family relationships and not just to comply with their wishes to control their child.

Aware that they had little support from relatives or friends, people welcomed confidential conversation with this outsider. Their realization that he would find time to see them, dropping in on some occasions, making specific arrangements to meet on others, was a surprise to people who had felt unworthy. As one mother expressed it:

> I felt so bad about my marriage breaking up, guilty you might say, that I didn't like to speak to anyone. I felt I'd be made to feel ashamed but I never had that feeling with Miss Pryce. . . . Before, I suppose, I thought it was checking up on children, say, children in broken marriages, but now I know she can be a friend, someone to depend on. . . .

Some sense of relationship with a social worker contrasted with feelings of isolation from other people, as with a middle-aged man released from prison and living in an unfamiliar city; the disabled mother of a 'difficult teenager' who had felt previously she could only call on the police; a teenage girl evicted from home whose friends were in a similar predicament. Meetings with each worker often made people feel better about themselves. Those who had spoken of valuing their independence now welcomed some dependence, albeit temporary, on this outsider. Far from being shameful, meeting some interested individual who visited without their asking was rewarding. It enabled people to discard previous beliefs that this official was 'just someone from the welfare' or, if he was still seen as someone from the welfare, that aspect of his job was of little consequence. In discussing their predicament with a social worker they had not felt like deviants. Although staff had provided visible resources, cash loan, place in a hostel, the most common change was in these clients' reinterpretation of social work and their associated reappraisal of themselves. As one man put it, 'When I first went to Mr Sawyer, I thought I was begging. After a time I realized I wasn't.'

Believing people to have 'relationship difficulties', workers found occasion to reactivate their reliance on helping by counselling, by listening and being listened to. They assumed that implementing such 'treatment' would involve encouraging interviewees to share their belief in its value. Each professional was proselytizing his definition of the situation, playing a missionary role (Balint 1963). Given that the clients had no other people or places to withdraw to, the worker was likely to gain converts to his idea that they would benefit from continued as well as immediate support.

In addition to people's changing feelings, there was other evidence of the success of such missions. Some clients had become resources to agencies, taking a voluntary job to redecorate old people's homes, becoming a short-term foster parent or home help. Such experiences widened individuals' interpretations of help and their awareness of what was involved in obtaining it. At the end of six months they described what each worker had meant to them and distinguished his role from that of other officials. They discussed generally the sorts of problems for which intervention might be appropriate and the behaviour which might disqualify others from receiving help. Mary (as in the above study) no longer regarded a social worker as someone concerned merely to control behaviour. She also claimed to have changed her friends' views on the subject.

When I first went there I thought social work was for people in trouble. You think that by looking at the newspapers. They say things like . . . 'pending social reports'. That's what my mates think it is, somebody to check on people in trouble.

Fifty-year-old Mr Taylor, an ex-prisoner, described what help from a social worker had meant to him.

He handled accommodation, he got me a place in the lodging house and then in the convalescent hospital. He knows when I'm avoiding him and when I'm not telling the truth. He's that sort of man. He's plain talking but he's the sort of guy who would go outside himself to help, whereas that chap they sent me to in Dundee two years ago, he wouldn't go two yards.

Conversion to workers' points of view about important goals in their occupation also helped dispel clients' anxieties and some stereotype ideas. A young woman who, as part of her worker's plans, had joined a single mother's weekly coffee-club run by the voluntary agency, explained.

I really found out about Miss Coulson. When she's there she's not like a social worker. There's a lot of folk think you've got to watch what you say to them but the way she spoke, now when she was speaking about life, she even talked about *Last Tango in Paris*. She was just the same as you, just a person with her own thoughts. A lot more people should go to these meetings.

At the end of a year another single mother described what had been involved in her changing relationship with 'her caseworker'.

I'd say people who don't put their trust in social workers never give them a chance. . . . It's really, though, the persons themselves who have to help themselves. Don't get me wrong, I'm not speaking as though she's an angel. She's no angel. If she thinks you are genuine she'll help you. If she thinks you are fussing about then I'm afraid you are climbing up the wrong tree. She wouldn't be slow in backing down on you and telling you exactly what she thinks.

Emphasis on the purpose and commitment required to counsel people with relationship-type problems was implicit in these workers' ideology of casework. Their sense of mission began by their interpreting problems as having to do with personal crises and their tasks as open-ended, having no obvious time limit. In their eyes this legitimated their initial intervention. Their interest was reinforced by respondents' appreciation. The latter's ability to distinguish a social-worker role from that of other officials and their often jargonistic accounts of the meaning of help illustrate conversion to the professionals' views that interpersonal support involved, ultimately, helping people to help themselves.

Not helped

In contrast to the careers of the above 'long-term clients' others' experiences were characterized by little or no coordination of activities. Although a worker began by assuming there was more to these people than met the eye, what he thought there was more of, and the problems and solutions which met the eye of the individuals concerned, were either dissimilar or were not viewed in the same light simultaneously: on meeting, they were thinking of different things. For example, one individual acknowledged having been depressed in the past, yet when she met the social worker she no longer accepted this condition as *a* problem or *the* problem. Suspicion of mental illness was the professional's frame of reference and the reason for his intervention. In these circumstances, negotiations hardly began because each party had different starting points, neither catching up with the other or being concerned about the same things for long enough to agree about an agenda, to establish ground rules for current exchanges let alone future ones.

The following case study concerns 26 year-old Mrs May who had left her husband and two children and moved to the city to start a new job. She was living with a Mr Williams who was separated from his wife. Mrs May had not accepted permanent separation from her own children and was anxious as to how Mr Williams's two children were adjusting to her.

According to the researcher's records the case included several problems: health, because this woman had taken an overdose of sleeping tablets; interpersonal, because she and Mr Williams were questioning whether they could together look after his children; unemployment, because Mrs May did not want to be financially dependent on Mr Williams; legal, because Mrs May wanted custody of her children but had little idea about legal procedures. The worker's task involved not so much interpreting a problem as defining all the problems together, their levels and priorities in the perceptions of client and social worker and their inter-relationships (Rees 1974). This was made even more difficult by a confusing route of referral.

Mrs May came to the notice of an area team via a letter signed by a 'medical assistant'. This 'assistant' turned out to be the psychiatrist who had interviewed Mrs May during her three days in hospital following an overdose of sleeping tablets. The psychiatrist's letter was posted a week after the patient's discharge and had been written without Mrs May's knowledge. It was addressed to the Director and eventually passed to a 'front-line' worker. He was unable to visit Mrs May for another two weeks, a delay of almost one month since she entered hospital. However, the picture painted by the psychiatrist's letter was fresh in his mind. That letter said:

> Her problems are mainly social and [therefore] it would be neces-sary to get one of your department involved. . . . I formed the impression that this was an inadequate psychopathic girl who was quite likely to take further overdoses but for whom hospitalization and psychiatric care had nothing to offer. I felt that she needed some supervision at home and that your department would be able to cope with it.

'Coping' was to depend on Mrs May's cooperation and her guesses about the purpose of the worker's surprise arrival on her doorstep.

> I don't remember seeing a social worker in the hospital. I thought they must be someone who was helping mothers who couldn't cope with kids . . . people who didn't have enough money, sort of thing, to cope with them.

The worker's frame of reference was different.

> We have of course a woman referred to us from the hospital as a result of taking an overdose. So we are concerned from that account and concerned with doing what we can to prevent her doing this again.

He explained his objectives.

> I'm not very good at making goals but one is to help her to express her feelings about this matter. I think mentally she needs to do that. She's not talking to anybody very much. I don't think she's talking to her cohabitee.

The worker didn't think it wise to be involved at that stage in Mrs May's struggle over the custody of her children.

> There's not much we can really do with couples who are fighting over their children. We could write to the social-work department where her husband lives but they would write back and say, 'This is not one of our problems, this is really a legal matter'.

Mrs May made sense of the worker's role in terms of experiences preceding and immediately following estrangement from her husband. Although nervous of her family doctor's attitude, she had sought his advice. 'He gave Bill a good "bollocking", put the fear of death into him'. She had also visited a 'social worker' who turned out to be a DHSS clerical officer. She reported his reaction – 'Go for your kids if he doesn't give you any money'. She sought police advice but they had not wanted to get involved 'provided the kids were looked after'. Some months after setting up a new home with Mr Williams a letter arrived from the RSPCC saying that they had heard (anonymously from a neighbour) that his children were not being properly looked after.

Following a second visit two weeks after the first, the worker wrote to Mrs May's husband about arrangements for visiting their children. The worker's allocation of time was affected by certain considerations.

> If I'm up that way I might call in. If I'm not up that way I'll probably not go until I get a reply from her husband or something has come up. I'm not quite at the unhappy state where I have clients who get neglected altogether, who might as well not be on the caseload. Sometimes I think I get a bit near it. When you are a student you do your best work because you are not pressed.

Within two months of the worker's first visit, Mrs May saw a solicitor regarding custody of her children. She was not sure of this person's interest and hoped the social worker would contact the lawyer and/or give his opinion on her chances of regaining custody of the children and how long the procedures would take.

> I said to the social worker would he be coming up again and he said yes. He said he would see the lawyer. I don't mind as long as I know I'm going to get my kids. I'm annoyed with this lawyer. I feel I've been running round in circles and nobody has moved . . . you feel with this lawyer, for instance, he is just young, he can't be any older than me. I want to know what he's doing and he never seems to know anything. It's unfair, nobody seems to know what my rights are. I sit here and argue with Jim. Half the land must hear us. Probably a lawyer or a social worker is telling my husband his rights. You need maybe someone not to tell you definite but to give you a fair idea of how you stand because you are frightened to make a move in case you are wrong. This young lawyer will turn round and say, 'You can do this and you can do that, but don't quote me on it'.

The passage of time settled some difficulties. Mrs May had initially pretended to neighbours that she was a housekeeper but had not liked the pretence and had found it unnecessary when she became friendly with other women in the block of flats. They became an indispensable source of support. In the next six months, she received unexpected visits from a housing visitor allegedly investigating Mr Williams's 'illegal' sub-letting; private detectives sent by her ex-husband; a representative of the RSPCC sent apparently by her cohabitee's previous wife.

The social worker telephoned the lawyer and confirmed that the latter had no idea how long a decision would take regarding custody. The worker was surprised at Mrs May's outward calmness and increasing resignation at the prospect of not regaining her children, yet he planned to 'watch the family' in order to anticipate any repetition of events which led to the initial referral. She guessed that this was what he had in mind when he visited unexpectedly at the end of six months.

> I wondered why he was coming. He seems to think I'm going to take another dose of pills. When he comes it's embarrassing because he doesn't seem to know what to say. . . . It seems ungrateful for me to say this but actually none of them seems able to do very much.

Some aspects of Mrs May's circumstances had changed since the psychiatrist had written his letter. But her haziness about the social worker's purpose remained. Such confusion was part of a pattern in this mother's meetings with significant others, including her doctor, the psychiatrist, the lawyer, the housing visitor, the private detectives, the visitor from the RSPCC. Their interviews with Mrs May may have served their needs but not always hers. She did not take such exchanges for granted yet had little control over them. Some resulted in frustration or fear, because it was not always clear where people had come from or what they could do. It was relatively easy for a social worker to become entangled in such a web, his function perceived as insignificant, little different from these others'.

The social worker's unplanned half-a-dozen visits stretching over a year had involved the kind of meetings which I have depicted elsewhere as 'no more than contact' because they were 'flirting and fleeting, transitory, not having much effect on a client's problem, their appreciation of the social worker's identity, their understanding of his job or their conception of themselves'. Such meetings had not included any obvious agenda for clarifying each party's assumptions about or responsibility towards the other (Rees 1974).

Other examples

Other cases in this casework-ideology 'not helped' category included three defined originally by workers and sources of referral as involving supervision of young people because information indicated that parents, school or police 'were concerned'. A large family, referred by a health visitor as having financial difficulties including rent arrears, was seen as having children with school-attendance problems. A young, pregnant mother, separated from her husband, was regarded by a social worker as requiring help in adjusting to admission to a mother-and-baby home and isolation from her family.

In some cases, following first interviews each party had different assumptions about the issue meriting most attention, as when a worker described his concern with a father's 'rejection' of his teenage son and the father hoped the worker would 'drum some sense into my boy'. In other cases different assumptions emerged later, as when people understood reasons for first meetings but not subsequent ones, or after initial visits didn't know why they had not seen the worker for some time. In these circumstances, layman and professional interpreted differently the purpose and duration of contact, and the former doubted the social worker's credibility as a helpful person.

It was argued earlier that when staff perceived a new request as being related to financial relief, unless other circumstances enabled them to reinterpret their task, they managed such work in one or two meetings. By contrast, when workers regarded 'requests' as involving relationship-type problems, they were more likely, for ideological reasons, to be at pains to avoid underestimating someone's difficulty. Some people, however, had one interpretation of help in mind and resisted the notion that the worker's intervention could be helpful in other ways: the mother who said she only wanted somewhere to live before her baby was born, the family who regarded their son's delinquency as 'one of those things'. In these circumstances workers' visits derived meaning as events in a kaleidescope of taken-for-granted meetings with others. People had some degree of trust in their association with known and not so well known local functionaries. The mother of a boy referred to the local authority by a headmaster:

> I'd no idea about social workers but we didn't mind seeing him if it would help. I'm a hairdresser . . . part-time . . . people come into the house a lot. The school officer's[6] always going around and he knows just to come into the house. . . . Our uncle is always here whether I'm here or not. I mean, as I say, the house is always open, anybody can come in. They always write down that they've been or called.

The social worker wanted to obtain a fuller picture of the family. His attention to detail – speculating about several unknown aspects of relationships – contrasted with these parents' assumptions that 'the problem' would resolve itself. The parents regarded their son's delinquency as not too unusual for boys of his age; he was being led by other allegedly more deliquent youths and the matter could be dealt with by spelling out what would happen if he did not mend his ways.

Ambiguity over intervention often showed in different interpretations of specific meetings, as when one worker was seen by a family as coming to collect rent but he himself regarded this as an opportunity to discuss the possibility of the father getting a job and to check the welfare of the children, whom he suspected of being maltreated. Different assumptions about the purpose and duration of social work dated sometimes from first interviews. Asked after one meeting how long she expected her association with the social worker would last, a mother replied, 'Well, tonight might finish it'. The worker's answer to the same question:

> I tend to see this as casework when I'm working with a family with a boy under supervision. Obviously there is going to be no short-term solution to these problems and the difficulties at school. He is not suddenly going to control his temper. . . .

In other long-term cases, mutual feelings of liking apparently became the means if not the ends of the association. Difficulties in articulating a particular purpose were not crucial if a worker was seen as a helpful person. If he was not quickly perceived in this light, it became difficult to convey interest, difficult to obtain later any explicit understanding about a problem or division of responsibilities. During interviews, individuals complied in the sense that workers did not regard them as having raised objections or questions. They received few clues about a family's feelings towards them, yet they asked people to call to see them again or paid brief visits themselves.

People commented critically about social workers as individuals when they found them difficult to speak to and were themselves uneasy about the extent of their authority. They were aware they were being assessed. They wanted to be well thought of and to know the social worker's feelings and intentions. Young people were anxious about a social worker's powers. Some parents saw their failure to effect improvement in their child's behaviour as resulting possibly in his 'prosecution' or as a last resort in his being removed from home.

Difficulty in communication stemmed from reactions to the worker as a person and a sense of powerlessness because people were not sure what was happening. They saw this 'official' as

uncertain, his style possibly represented his attitude towards them:
his reservedness indicating reservations about the truth of what
they had told him, his distance indicating doubts about their
ability to manage their circumstances or their children. With
responsibilities which they regarded as open-ended, the social
workers were not so much uncertain about what to do but rather
ambivalent about interviewing at all. As one social worker put it:

> Probably the more information you got in a case like this, the more
> help you can be . . . But I made it very clear that I wasn't there to
> interfere.

Although initially interested in people who appeared to be
suffering personal stress, workers ceased to regard such cases as a
priority if people responded to situations of personal stress and
discomfort indifferently. They did not want to disturb their
schedule merely to follow up people who appeared uncom-
municative, or unwilling clients in other respects. One social
worker anticipated such developments.

> The difficulty comes after you've had a case six weeks because then
> you're getting new cases which you have to deal with and so the ones
> you've had inevitably get less attention.

'Inevitably get less attention', was explained:

> In the first few months you are conscious if you are going to be able
> to help. . . . If you are getting a response you think this person is
> wanting help, then you rate it higher. If you get the type of person
> who really doesn't want to see you and you don't feel you are getting
> anywhere, you tend to put it lower down.

In agency records such cases represented 'voluntary supervision',
'casework with single parents'. Staff remained concerned but
expected future meetings to be infrequent unless individuals went
out of their way to indicate that they needed 'help' or brought
themselves to the worker's attention in other ways. Staff participated in a self-fulfilling prophecy. Without encouragement,
even 'personal dependency' cases diminished quickly in importance in relation to other work. Clients were unlikely to
change their initial feelings of ambiguity about this person and
their perception of his role in their lives as marginal.

People who shared the value placed on helping people to help
themselves thus reinterpreted their own role in such a context and
learned something of the private world of the professional. By
contrast, those who were unaware of a particular worker's purpose
remained confused about social work generally. Given the passage
of six months and changing events, such as one girl losing her job
and being involved in what parents described as renewed

deliquency, a mother's gradual acceptance that she might not regain custody of her children, an unmarried mother's marriage, a death in another family, a social worker's interest was forgotten or regarded as insignificant. Parents or teenage children had new experiences to make sense of and although reappraising themselves and their current circumstances, they made little connection between these and the interest of the person in their case. A youth placed originally on voluntary supervision recalled the social worker as one of several visitors such as a 'friendly, plain-clothes detective', the school welfare officer and the researcher.[7] Three months after being placed under compulsory supervision by a Children's Hearing, and nine months after his original referral, the same 14 year-old boy was unsure what had happened.

> Do you mind telling me, Sir, whether I'm on probation. . . . I've not seen him for ages and I'm not sure whether I'm supposed to see him or not. . . . When he did come he just asked about school and things that went wrong before. . . . I thought he was coming to see me, let me know what I had to do.

The worker explained why he had not seen the youth and why he might also limit meetings in similar cases.

> After you've worked with a family you begin to feel that there is not much more you can do. Therefore, maybe after a year they sort of close themselves out . . . for better or worse.

Following the birth of her child a mother, separated from her husband and living temporarily in a mother-and-baby home, had avoided the social worker, despite invitations to visit.

> I stopped going to see her. She was a bit like me, quiet. I didn't think she was doing much anyway. If I had to do all this over again I'd rather get back on friendly terms with my folks than see the social worker.

Of the same situation the social worker commented:

> I wanted something useful to come from her living through this experience. . . . I lost contact. I'm not particularly satisfied but I don't feel it was all my own fault. She was pretty unwilling to come forward with lots of things. At the home we spoke about all the other girls and you could never get her back to herself. . . .

In spite of workers' sense of mission about desirable long-term objectives, they were unable to convert respondents to their point of view. Some social workers felt a responsibility to support and counsel people yet regarded them as elusive to find at home or to communicate with generally. From clients' points of view, the worker was seldom seen, or not seen for long enough to be able to establish some relationship. Meetings ceased. Cases were kept open for periods of up to six months and for as long as a year but these clients experienced a sense of ambiguity over the initial grounds for intervention. They viewed the worker's role as always marginal and as time passed increasingly hazy.

Summary

Whether clients were helped by social workers did not depend merely on the availability of resources. Rather, resources were interpreted so as to match aspects of social workers' ideologies. For example, in cases regarded routinely as low in priority, social workers felt that the responsibility for finding remedies was not theirs. Faced with the problems of people in whom they were very interested, they used their time creatively and worked at producing solutions even though none seemed obvious.

Case management influenced by the operation of ideologies of service and relief, was controlled by social workers. They liked to provide quickly a relatively simple service to clients whose problems they understood and which seemed unusual for these people. In these face-to-face encounters and from some clients' points of view, either you got help or you did not. There were exceptions to this rule, as in relationships which began with promise but in which social workers' interest slipped. Regarding clients who hoped for immediate material relief of some kind and who received no help, several circumstances combined to effect social workers' decisions that there was nothing they could do: sources of referral had not given a precise picture of these people's problems; social workers felt that the clients were used to difficulties of some kind and did not seem very willing to help themselves; even if the clients sensed that social workers had misunderstood or underestimated their problems, they did not elaborate about themselves or their requests but acquiesced passively in being turned away.

A second type of case management was characterized by the social worker's adherence to routine procedures for providing a service which involved getting to know the clients. The social workers explained that they expected to have several meetings to enable them to discover whether people should be passed as entitled to some 'resource', as in obtaining a place in a day-care centre for mentally handicapped children, or in being passed as prospective adoptive parents. The client applicants' knowledge that they could expect to be interviewed on several occasions acted as an incentive to anticipate the content of future meetings and an opportunity to learn more about social work. They could prepare to raise topics and introduce other people to the social worker. They not only enlarged their experience of how social workers operated but also raised their expectations of the help they needed. A few turned down facilities and other offers of help. Their meetings with a social worker had enabled them to work out alternative ways of coping.

A third type of case management involved social workers in advocating the value of casework objectives. They welcomed the prospect of meeting people who were experiencing several problems, including rejection by relatives, and who gave the impression that they would benefit from talking out their difficulties and formulating plans to make changes in their management of their lives, not least in their personal relationships. Such social work intervention was successful when a client was converted to a social worker's view that the most desirable means and ends of social work involved helping people to help themselves. In fulfilling such objectives, social workers exercised controls. They also provided support through friendship and resources such as money, accommodation and access to other personnel including home helps and volunteer visitors.

Despite a sense of mission, social workers were not always successful in their attempts to attain casework objectives. Several clients did not feel helped. Some social workers were clumsy in pushing their point of view. They did not sense that clients' expectations of the helping process were different from theirs. Other social workers felt a concern for clients yet were ambivalent about being seen to intervene too openly. In consequence clients perceived them as uncertain or as not really interested. Personal incompatability between clients and social workers resulted. The things which were on clients' minds, such as everyday tasks and the accumulation of new difficulties, did not match the social workers' initial grounds for intervention. Their continued sense of responsibility for a case was pointless unless they took account of clients' new concerns and revised their objectives accordingly.

Running through social workers' several ideologies were assumptions about worthy and unworthy tasks and, at least by implication, deserving and undeserving clients. This theme also concerned clients, as in their references to what it meant to them to have to experience certain problems and seek help. Such value judgements emerged in the context of different client/social worker relationships. The links between such moral evaluations and the outcome of clients' meetings with social workers are the subject of discussion in the next chapter.

NOTES

1 One case not included in this typology began with a social worker defining a family's problem as 'overcrowding' and her task as enabling them to be rehoused. This was achieved within a few months and mostly on that social worker's initiative. At this point she was succeeded by a colleague who resisted having the same role as his predecessor. The father and his family did not keep appointments with the second social worker and eventually left the area without the worker's knowledge. In one sense the work demonstrated the service ideals of the first social worker and her success, in cooperation with other officials, in obtaining accommodation. Judged at six months, however, the case represented an attempt to engage in long term casework which did not materialize. The improvements effected by one worker were short lived. The family left the area before we could ask them for their assessment of the social workers' intervention overall.
2 Reference to the scheme introduced in 1971 to supplement the low income of those in full-time work and with at least one child. See Lynes, T., *The Penguin Guide to Supplementary Benefits*, London, Penguin 1972.
3 This was a reference to the location of the city's main Supplementary Benefits Office.
4 Negotiations about such criteria are discussed in Chapter 5, pp. 126–8.
5 Criteria affecting decisions 'in the best interests of a child' are discussed in Chapter 5.
6 Refers to the educational welfare officer from the Education Dept.
7 In spite of what we regarded as clarification, the family regarded the interviewer as 'something to do with social work'. In this respect the interviewer was another official whom they had to make sense of.

Clients' and Social Workers' Search for Moral Character

> Whenever the welfare of one person potentially depends upon the actions of another the latter may face a moral decision. It is only with awareness of this dependence that the process of moral decision making can commence
>
> (Schwartz 1970).

Introduction

The meetings between the social workers and their respective clients have shown that the provision of 'help' depended on the ability of the layman to project and the professional to recognize worthy 'moral character'. To each social worker these features constituted evidence that such clients merited his commitment of time and the provision of other appropriate 'resources'. By contrast, some people were considered unworthy. Social workers felt little, if any, obligation to help.

In elaborating this conclusion that the social workers' interpretations of people and their problems as worthy or unworthy were the criteria determining the outcome of negotiations, I will repeat information about the clients' feelings on being referred, the conditions affecting the development of the staff's ideologies and some examples from the case studies. My objectives are to highlight the processes leading to people being judged deserving, less deserving or undeserving *and* to account for the moral character of decision making in social work as a whole.

Although my concern is to focus attention on the use of moral criteria by the clients *and* the social workers, we should not overlook the historical and societal context in which these criteria were located. This social work was being practised in a society with a particular economic system and with certain values. To put it mildly, there was and is, political uncertainty about the ethical and actuarial justification for providing social services as a universal benefit for citizens who could not have purchased them with their money in an open market. To put it strongly, there was and is widespread antagonism towards poor people who are thought to be unjustifiably dependent on a range of 'welfare services'. In times of national economic recession this antagonism has amounted to a welfare backlash. Every country with a similar economic system and which sponsors social services through general taxation, tries to resolve these issues, often publicly, as in politicians' pronouncements about the desirable hallmarks of national policies. Members of the general public have hoped or assumed that in their lives they would enjoy some economic self-sufficiency, the support of their families and general good health, that only unfortunate or deviant people would not have these experiences. In consequence, the allocation of resources, even in the personal social services, was believed to depend on the ability of administrators and others to distinguish between groups of citizens, to sort out the guilty from the innocent, the responsible from the irresponsible (Glastonbury *et al.* 1973; Rees and Atkison 1978). The rationale which government and voluntary agencies had used since the turn of the century to assess needy people's eligibility for various kinds of help was a legacy which influenced the practices of present-day social workers. In this respect the past was being rewritten in social work: age-old beliefs about a society's need to separate the deserving from the undeserving poor still affected the outcomes of these social worker/client relationships, which, in other respects, had some very different characteristics.

Moral decision-making in other contexts

Before elaborating clients' and social workers' criteria of 'moral character' and the types of relationships from which they evolved, it will be useful to leave social work temporarily and show that such a process of decision making is not peculiar to these personal service organizations. Making decisions on the basis of some people being considered worthy of attention and others unworthy, or not worthy, occurs when professionals are employed in positions of power and privilege to ration resources, to categorize people on a basis of need or blame, of appropriate or inappropriate behaviour (Becker 1963). Such decisions are made usually with reference to routines of practice familiar to these employees and the recipients are relatively powerless, almost at their mercy. Examples of this process of selecting and sieving people on the basis of what may seem arbitrary criteria but which reflect some typology familiar to the professionals, arise from different periods of history, different walks of life, and vary in the seriousness of the consequences for the groups of individuals thus labelled. For example, the notion of triage was used in the First World War to sort wounded soldiers into groups, providing medical aid for those likely to survive if treated immediately, identifying others who would get better without medical help and leaving the rest to their fate. Soldiers who received treatment were usually thought to have chances not only of living but also of fighting again. Adapted to the world food situation the system of triage has involved directing aid to those nations thought likely to have a reasonable chance of survival and leaving others to starve (Knightley 1975).

Life and death consequences also follow from medical personnel's definition of a situation, as when staff in hospital emergency rooms categorize some patients as socially derogatory and morally unworthy of maximum life-saving treatment (Sudnow 1967). In the administration of justice, assessments of 'character' affect intervention in people's lives as when police decide whether to search or arrest suspicious persons (Sachs 1972). Distinctions between serious delinquents, 'good boys' and misguided youths and the outcomes of these assessments have been described as depending on police appraisal of youths' personal characteristics and not their offences, which were similar (Briar and Piliavin 1964). Probation officers in American juvenile courts define the moral character of offenders by weighing the presence or absence of circumstances associated with serious delinquency, including previous offences, the demeanour of an offender and the attitudes of parents (Emerson 1969). In a London magistrate's court the divergence between the posited absolute morality of professionals' ethics and the situated morality of their actual activities was minimized by these professionals (police, lawyers, probation officers) arguing, 'this is what any reasonable man would do in this situation'. Such a court of law, like a theatre, was an arena in which the character of the defendants reflected rules emanating from relationships between court and legal personnel (Carlen 1976). Regarding English supplementary-benefits claimants' experiences before appeals tribunals, it was allegedly difficult to escape the conclusion that it was the appellant's psychological make-up and cultural life style that was being judged (Rose 1973). Decisions about rehousing Glasgow tenants were influenced by that city's Housing Department counter-staff's impressions of tenants and by housing visitors' reports. These included criteria which I would regard as 'non-moral' such as notes about individual tenants' preferences and their lengh of tenancy, but also notes about their record of rent arrears and a grading of people on the basis of criteria such as 'type of people', 'cleanliness', 'furniture'. In one area visits for these grading purposes lasted two or three minutes and some people were graded according to what was 'known' about them and without their being seen (Jacobs 1975).

The concern with moral character is not confined to those in positions of power. The tenants just referred to were described as often hurriedly tidying and even redecorating their homes in the hope of being well graded. Concern with 'healthy independence' is part of the process affecting the use of social and health services. People recognize problems yet avoid seeking help because of the stigma associated with being less than self-sufficient. In America the use of mental health services had moral implications and tended to be stigmatized by the average layman (Phillips 1963). The use of income-support services in Britain, Ireland and the United States was regarded by groups eligible for such support as stigmatizing, a factor which partially explains the low take-up of entitlements, in particular those involving means-tested benefits (Meacher 1973; Clifford 1975; Horan and Austin 1974; Beck 1967). In Britain, even people who suffered coronary heart diseases were still apt to make moral judgements of themselves and others as to whether they should seek financial or even medical help – one third of all respondents, including coronary heart patients, acutely sick bronchitics and controls, saying that seeking any financial aid was bad for the individual's self-respect (Pinker 1974).

Moral character in social work

In the following discussion 'moral' has the connotation deserving, not so deserving, undeserving. It refers to value judgements about people and their problems which affected the actions of social workers *and* clients. It does not refer to any absolute set of principles guiding workers' actions, or to any set of specific rights which consumers could learn of and try to obtain. On the contrary, what social workers felt they *ought* to do or clients felt they should be entitled to was relative to the constraints of knowledge, traditions and assumptions about resources. These constraints operated in social work as a whole and with reference to one of three contexts. Contexts refer to the types of case management which resulted from the operation of particular staff ideologies.

'Character' will refer sometimes to the commonly accepted dictionary definition of some individual's personal characteristics, such as an aspect of their reputation based on current interpretations of information about their past. Sometimes 'character' will be used to refer to routine aspects of a social worker's task as defined by that practitioner and his colleagues. More often than not this concept means a synthesis of these considerations, a judgement of an individual in relation to his problems in a particular context of social work. Thus, moral character could reflect some judgement about respectability but only in relation to whatever is being assessed (Ball 1970). It was conditional on the assumptions about different types of meetings, not something permanent and fixed but rather an assessment 'which holds until further notice' (Schutz 1962). Case outcomes were affected by the interplay between practical contingencies and the processual and conditional nature of value judgements which were the hub of decisions. In some cases the social workers and their clients were explicit about their moral calculations. In other cases these criteria were not so easy to discern because of attention given to other topics. For example, social workers stressed some other constraints which affected their performance of their jobs: technical ones (e.g. their knowledge of resources); professional ones (e.g. their assumptions about appropriate roles for trained staff); extra-organizational ones (e.g. the pressures from other agencies). The social workers' use of value judgements were intertwined with these other considerations and difficult to disentangle from them.

Before analysing how value judgements emerged as bases for the social workers' decisions and the clients' reactions to them I want to refer again to some events in the social workers' and clients' worlds and in particular to the influence of ideologies on the social workers' power to control their involvement with clients.

The social workers' world

Several conditions affected the social workers' management of their time in general and their roles in particular cases. In this social work they had discretionary powers. There were few written or statutory rules to which they had to adhere.

Operationalizing agency traditions and policies influenced their assessment of priorities. They held assumptions about desirable roles for social workers, about rewarding work, about resources being almost always available in some cases and usually unavailable in others. They made sense of these job issues through the development of practice-oriented ideologies, those sets of ideas about categories of cases and means of dealing with them. These incorporated work routines, typified people's problems and staff's roles. They enabled the staff to manage what most regarded as an occupational hazard of having large caseloads and too little time and other resources to deal with them.

Other professional and bureaucratic considerations influenced staff decisions whether and how quickly to intervene. For example, their interpretations of someone's problem often took shape before face-to-face contact and this explained why some people had limited knowledge of the grounds and agenda of that first meeting. Often unknown to the individual concerned, sources of referral suggested the desirability of a social workers' intervention and something specific about its purpose. Staff assumptions about outside parties' motives influenced their attitudes, the first inference about someone's credentials being derived from appraisal of the status and credibility of the source of referral. For example, social workers thought health visitors had a habit of taking action for the sake of it, to meet their own needs to be seen to do something on a family's behalf. Such referrals were regarded sceptically, as not necessarily indicating evidence of a serious problem. By contrast, doctors in a children's hospital were less likely to pass on people and information unnecessarily. Social workers made these distinctions because referrals from hospital medical staff were infrequent by comparison with the larger number of cases passed on by health visitors. It was also a reflection of the status attributed to paediatricians and their habit of writing a letter to the Director of Social Work describing a problem and what help might be required. In the first instance, in these cases, social workers were assessing the referral agents' moral character not the prospective clients'.

The clients' world

The moral character of seeking help was also of concern to clients. Their feelings about self-respect and the importance of having grounds for believing they had earned the help of others affected their attitudes towards local authority or voluntary agency. A source of ideas about entitlements and the moral connotation of being referred derived from relatives and, less often, from friends and acquaintances. People in an individual's personal network passed on information about their experiences at the hands of voluntary and statutory 'social service agencies'. They related how they had been received and what help they had obtained. Others told what they had heard about the functions of such agencies. For example, parents passed on to children items of local folklore about the income-maintenance and welfare functions of the voluntary agency. In addition to information from relatives and friends, people's views of how they might be treated by social workers were affected by the reactions of relatives to *their* (the client's) changed and often difficult circumstances. These included pre- or extra-marital pregnancy, the break-up of a marriage, the onset of some disability, the worsening of financial and housing difficulties. Contacting these agencies involved divulging information which they had not wished to share with members of their family. Sharing information with relatives had implied some dependence on family members, a position which people wished to avoid. Others anticipated that relations would be critically judgemental, indirectly and by inference and innuendo, or by openly disparaging remarks and other forms of rejection. Rather than risk such stigmatization they told no one of their difficulties.

The patterns of behaviour depicted in the clients' orientations to seeking help indicated that their encounters with those in positions of authority – such as supplementary-benefits officials, teachers, doctors, representatives of various local authority agencies – had made impressions which were not easily revised and coloured their view of social services in general. Specific unpleasant experiences, such as being treated abruptly, having to wait a long time in a public waiting room with 'less deserving' people before entitlement to supplementary benefit was assessed, had reinforced some clients' beliefs that seeking help involved some position of dependency, however temporary, and was not worth the risks of being turned away, or of having to place themselves in a powerless position in meetings with strange officials.

Other individuals' more hopeful views of social work were influenced by recollections of experiences with officials which were pleasant and encouraging, or at least not unpleasant and discouraging. This refers to those who had little or no experience of financial dependence, who had enjoyed regular employment and a predictable income. There were aspects of their past conduct, such as 'working all their lives', 'paying their taxes', 'never having been in trouble' and 'fighting for their country', which influenced their anticipation of 'getting a fair hearing'. They expected a social worker to take such worthy credentials into consideration even if they could not be sure that their view of their past conduct would be shared by this person and so influence the outcome of meetings.

The routes of referral and people's feelings about being referred indicated that many were reluctant clients. Most described some sense of shame over the problem which brought them to another's attention. Even the large minority who felt neutral about being referred showed that their reasons for feeling as they did were moral ones: they had usually been able to manage their own affairs. Therefore, they reasoned, they deserved help because they were not in the habit of asking for it.

Power relationships in specific contexts

Although the social workers made assumptions about their responsibilities in different types of cases, their assessments of worthiness or unworthiness were not entirely prejudged. Their interpretations of moral character evolved from and derived meaning from their interaction with the clients. This contention follows closely the thesis that moral meanings are 'socially constructed'; they require coordination or 'teamwork' between two or more persons, one being concerned to project himself as respectable, as morally acceptable, thereby prompting in the other an obligation to treat that person, in that current meeting, as someone entitled to those services which persons of this kind have a right to expect (Ball 1970; Goffman 1971). Regarding any individual client, a social worker's intervention was affected by his interpretation of several aspects of 'character', including information about past behaviour, reactions to physical appearance, people's verbal skills and other ways of responding, or a combination of all these things.

In negotiations about problems, staff usually exercised most power because they were familiar with conducting interviews, they had knowledge of resources and of criteria affecting their use. They could give or withhold information. The existence of such a power axis meant that an individual's ability to obtain the decision he required was limited, except in so far as he could make favourable impressions. Most interaction took place along this axis and affected the content and outcome of meetings. However, the social workers conducted different kinds of negotiations. In some cases there was little bargaining, clients had limited opportunity to learn of reasons for what occurred, irrespective of whether they had been helped. Such meetings as there were had some characteristics of auditions, a concept which I will discuss in a moment. In other meetings, clients were involved in sharing information, in discussing and learning about grounds for decisions. In these exchanges, criteria of moral character were explicit and negotiable. Other social work was intended by the staff to resemble a relationship between equals and, therefore, to guarantee a social worker's continued interest and support.

Of course, there were similarities between one interpersonal context of practice and another. For example, all first meetings had some characteristics of auditions. Both parties gave impressions to the other. Both were concerned to gain feedback about these. In some cases one or both wanted reassurance about the implications of offering and receiving help. Nevertheless, it is the differences which concern me. These rested on the power of the social worker to link value judgements to other conditions affecting his work and on the client's awareness of and participation in this process. These contexts and the considerations affecting each party's search for evidence of moral character can be described diagrammatically (Table 5.1) and will now be identified and compared. They reflect the influence of the social workers' ideologies and correspond to the types of case management outlined in the last chapter.

Auditions

A characteristic of auditions is that the performers are being given a trial hearing, they may not be sure of the criteria by which their performance is being assessed and they have a relatively short time in which to influence their assessors' opinion. Clients and social workers explained that many meetings did not last long and thus limited the former's opportunity to give an impression of their problems and influence a decision. Sometimes the experience of audition-type exchanges was the sum total of people's association with social workers, including those (pp. 62–7) whose verdict was that they had been helped.

In case management influenced by service and relief ideologies, people's appearances, what they said and their manner of saying it, affected outcomes. Although impressed by outward signs, staff did not react to appearances in isolation. They weighed the connection between problem and individual, between sets of circumstances and personal characteristics, between act and biography and interpreted such information in relation to familiar objectives and means of implementing them.

Reactions to appearances were linked intimately to one or a combination of several considerations including assumptions about the source of referral's motives and a worker's knowledge of and access to resources. However, some impression of an individual's independence relative to his current problem was

Table 5.1 Client/social worker experiences influencing the search for evidence of moral character

CLIENTS' WORLD: SEEKING HELP

SOCIAL WORKERS' WORLD: GIVING HELP

Experiences of education, employment, obtaining income	Training & related experiences
Attitudes to independence	Attitudes to independence
Family status, attitudes of relatives	Interpretations of agency functions

Orientation to seeking help

Practice oriented ideologies

CLIENT

SOCIAL WORKER

Negotiations: the cost of involvement

Search for moral character

Auditions
Shared information
Interdependence & alliance

Types of client/social worker relationships affecting impressions of moral character the aspect which most influenced staff actions. The question of dependency was most important, yet its effect on the outcome of meetings was unpredictable. For example, some individuals' accounts of their difficulties represented in staff eyes a deserving state of dependency meriting immediate help; the behaviour of others, though representing some condition of dependency, was seen as less deserving or as undeserving. The experiences of those whose requests were defined as deserving and for whom help was provided quickly, will be examined first.

'Deserving'
First meetings were an opportunity to obtain information, to confirm or confound impressions derived from the source of referral. On eventually meeting, it was apparently easy for clients to clarify requests seen by social workers as related to resources over which they had some control. In these cases the outcome appeared to hinge on a worker's knowledge of and access to items such as extra cash grant for a special diet, aids for the disabled, a vacancy in a nursery school, temporary holiday accommodation. But clients did not regard such help as a mechanical, taken-for-granted affair. Those receiving this service felt it necessary to convey that seeking help of any kind was relatively unusual for them and that the problem which had prompted the social worker's intervention was specific and limited. In cases of aged and disabled people, social workers saw evidence of these individuals' 'sensible management of their financial affairs', their otherwise good health and the support of relatives. Families could demonstrate worthiness by evidence of their reputation for caring for dependents, how in the past they had almost always been willing and able to help one another. For example, concerning Mrs Rose's request for temporary holiday accommodation for her aged father-in-law the social worker explained:
> I thought this was for the good of the whole family. It wasn't that Mrs Rose was trying to kick her father-in-law out.

Social workers were pleased to provide a relatively simple service to people who had maintained and valued their independence and were unlikely to make other demands. However, staff regarded some resources, such as accommodation of various kinds, as being at best in short supply – at worst they felt 'beat before you start'. Problems having been thus defined, the service required was unlikely to be provided immediately unless the worker perceived unusual or extenuating circumstances obliging him to redefine his objectives. Unless he did this, he felt powerless to do more than investigate briefly the client's means and other living conditions. For example, local authority staff regarded enquiries for vacancies in old people's homes as unimportant tasks involving little more than recording information for later processing on agency records. However, in one such apparently routine case the worker changed his assumption that there was little he could do except complete an administrative formality. His intervention on behalf of an old lady referred by her daughter-in-law was explained:

> The fact that she's had this nervous breakdown and been taken into Queenswells in the past indicates that she's in need of company and looking after. I just had the feeling that that little bedroom she was in that particular day seemed very much like a prison.

His appeal that this old lady was deserving was based on 'medical criteria'. He felt obliged to communicate this point of view to a senior colleague responsible for residential care, to stress that this case was in the 'very urgent' category.[1]

When social workers felt sorry for people, their ascription of worthiness to the latter emanated from this alliance of sympathy and not because the practitioner had easy access to some known resource. Regarding some old people, conditions of deserving dependency were thus defined as much by what people did not say as by what they did. In these circumstances even some degree of inarticulateness apparently had the effect of speaking louder than words. The social worker who saw an old lady's room as being 'like a prison' also recalled 'she was very reserved, she did not complain about anything'. Other staff who initially felt bound to try to 'support' two women recently widowed because the women had no available relatives, had also been impressed by these individuals' stoical tolerance of loneliness, by their uncomplaining management of what was presumed to be a sense of loss and grief. One social worker's sense of obligation was reinforced because, at the age of 59, the woman had missed by a few months the Prime Minister's £10 Christmas bonus for pensioners.

Two types of presentations of self have so far been described as influencing staff decisions to intervene quickly: clients who demonstrated their request was worth meeting by not being in the habit of asking for outsiders' help and in other current matters in their lives being able to manage for themselves; clients who were suddenly dependent but had not asked directly for any specific service. Another property of cases prompting that moral-quality decision, 'meriting swift intervention', lay in the social worker's concerns rather than 'worthy' characteristics attributed to the client. In staff eyes, professional and bureaucratic criteria made certain cases a high priority and 'compelled' them to take action. Some human predicaments were routinely defined as deserving because if things went wrong they could threaten a social worker's sense of his own personal worth, possibly even his job security. For example, the hint of suicide, evidence of previous history of mental illness, of children and young people being in moral and physical danger prompted social workers into fulfilling some watchdog, supervisory function, at least until they revised their inter- pretations. Almost by appearance alone a teenager impressed a worker into taking her into care with few questions asked because she was seen as 'otherwise going to drop'. Such 'crisis cases' were morally worthy of attention in the sense that staff took for granted the seriousness of their responsibility and did not want to risk the consequences of delaying help.

Special features of case management contributed to clients' audition-type experiences and affected the responses even of those who had received help. For example, a worker's apparent acceptance of someone's request acted as feedback to people about *their* worthiness; but little was made explicit and clients were unsure of the grounds of that interest. They contrasted their reception with what they regarded as their more peremptory treatment at the hands of other officials. The 59 year-old widow said, 'I don't know why he's taken this trouble over me but I'm just so grateful for all he's done.'[2] Another woman compared her meeting with a social worker to a rather different exchange with a Housing Department visitor.

The like of Mr B., I think you could ask him anything whether he could answer it or not. Other people are so abrupt you just wonder, should you ask. You don't mean anything against them but if people are abrupt you sometimes hold back.

The teenage girl who was immediately provided with temporary accommodation interpreted the social worker's action and atti- tude:

When I met her she was different. She treated me like a person whereas you're just a number at social security and they only deal with money.

Fulfilling objectives with only limited client participation pro- vided few opportunities for clients to redress the balance of what some saw as an unequal giver/receiver relationship, a situation out- side their control. Yet those who had been considered worthy of help wanted to reciprocate, in particular to avoid giving an im- pression of getting something for nothing. This dilemma, of being grateful for having been considered deserving, yet having few means of 'giving' something in return, could be managed. For example, those old people who had received physical aids referred neighbours for consideration for similar help and explained to the social worker the useful effect of his intervention. By avoiding appearing ungrateful they preserved some sense of identity and self-respect. Such expressions of gratitude were also reassuring to any worker who had doubts about the value of spending time on such work at the expense of other tasks.

'Undeserving'

Some clients' problems were not dealt with. Their interviews were terminated quickly, a not surprising outcome given the social workers' ideology of relief with its several unwritten rules why help should not be given.

My analysis of social workers' decisions being affected by clients' appearances showed staff making connections between clients' submissiveness and some risk of physical or mental illness. Passivity in interviews was not in itself interpreted as evidence of a serious predicament and did not always elicit a sense of obligation to intervene. In connection with a request for help with material difficulties such behaviour resulted in the social worker under-estimating the extent of someone's problems and deciding to carry his investigation no further. The careers of the 60 clients show that people who had hoped for assistance in the form of money or some material aid and who slanted their request to match what they regarded as the agency's relief-giving function, were among those with whom contact was quickly terminated. Social workers recalled these people as having given the impression that they thought the social worker would understand their situation with little elaboration from them. This, together with the fact that sources of referral were regarded as having an unclear purpose in advising the 'applicant' to go to the agency, became 'evidence' of the client's low motivation to change. This last was the catalyst ingredient effecting each worker's decision to limit his responsibility rather than improvise further.

In relation to material problems, other client attitudes were unlikely to result in staff initiatives and could be counter-productive. In contrast to the old lady who 'did not complain', it was apparently difficult to feel sympathy for those who 'moaned and expected you to work miracles', who were 'very demanding and manipulators' or who 'would have you running every minute of the day'. People who gave the impression that an agency was 'just a place for handouts', that they thought the only relationship in social work was of the giver-receiver kind, were conveying a view of the helping process which was ideologically unpalatable to most social workers. It was a point of view also disliked by clients who stressed that they expected to have earned an entitlement to help and did not want something for nothing.

Staff defined behaviour as off-putting not only as a result of immediate reactions to face-to-face encounters but also in relation to whether they thought people would be able to help themselves. In this last respect a social worker explained that a woman who was not in the sample influenced which characteristics she looked for in other old people wanting material help.

> There is one that annoys me, an old lady that lives in a new house. She won't spend her money, she won't buy food and she won't put on the fire and she sits about in her coat and gives her money to her drunken son, but deprives herself of food. She has annoyed me quite a lot.

However, the social workers' perceptions of certain problems as being of low priority and the individual clients as being unpromising to work with, were not built up only from reactions to people in interviews and recall of what had occurred in similar cases. These social workers were also influenced by their awareness of agency traditions and policies. These included guidelines that financial help should only be given if some specific goal was involved, such as preventing evictions and/or children being taken into care, preventing the possibility of nervous breakdown and/or supporting those who appeared as though they might achieve some state of independence in the future. Constrained by a policy which reflected other influences, such as the moral attitudes of elected lay councillors,[3] social workers were also selective to whom they gave cash help because of its possible effect on the expectations of others. Assessing a client's entitlement involved careful management of agency image and reputation. Helping one person unrealistically was thought by some staff – a point expressed by seniors at area team allocation meetings – as likely to result in word getting around a particular neighbourhood leading to an unmanageable number of other enquiries.

Regarding people who had not been helped and who, according to staff, had had little to say in interviews, there was little evidence that that experience was compounded by any feelings of self-rejection. It did not assume any great importance. They were not critical. They did not feel they had been openly rejected. Of their polite reception and the equally pleasant way in which they left empty-handed, some said this proved 'you'd best keep yourself to yourself', others said they hadn't wished to cause trouble, that, in one case, the social worker's civility showed that she had 'done her best' even though the worker conceded she had been able to do nothing. One old person felt dissuaded from trying again. A Mrs McKay said of the suggestion that she should investigate her entitlement at the supplementary benefits offices before returning to the voluntary agency,

> I wouldn't want to go there again because they've a lot to do. I wouldn't want to be a nuisance to anybody but it was her [the health visitor] who told me you might get help. He [her husband] is not well and, oh, you wonder if it's worth carrying on.

Staff thought some people were manipulators or overdemanding, yet there was no open conflict in interviews and the client was left to speculate on the reasons behind the social worker's action. Their explanations why they had not been helped reflected general assumptions about the functioning of 'the welfare' or of 'social work': that getting help was a matter of chance; that only undeserving people got help; that social workers operated a points system somewhat like housing departments. As one man who had been referred elsewhere put it,

> Seemingly you have to have your name down on the books for some time before they'll look at you.

This interpretation corresponded to a senior social worker's opinion,

> Only when voluntary cases become known are they able to move up the priority list, they gain more points as it were.

In further interviews with the same or with another social worker these people might have demonstrated that their difficulties were unusual for them or were unusual compared to what the interviewing social worker knew of clients with similar problems. Unless they did this they had little chance of changing the social worker's view of their credentials, of redeeming the bad reputation established in first meetings. For those quickly defined as unworthy – for the sort of reasons discussed above – their experience and its outcome were analogous to an unsuccessful audition. The client – as hopeful but anxious performer – has not made a good impression. The social worker, as busy, perhaps harassed impresario, has ended the contact with an implicit 'don't ring us, we'll ring you', which was usually euphemistically expressed as in invitations to call again if they thought it would be helpful, or in advice to contact some other agency.

Managing uncertainty

Interpretations of moral character were not established only from first impressions nor were decisions to try to help always made immediately following first meetings. Social workers often reserved judgement until they had investigated matters further and on the basis of extra information could confirm or confound earlier, tentative or ambivalent feelings towards this person and his predicament. In some cases social workers' initial ambivalent feelings were replaced by a sense of clarity and commitment; in others, initial staff uncertainty was resolved when they felt discouraged from taking further action. Regarding the latter, some people did not take up a worker's invitation to visit on a second occasion or they failed to keep appointments. In other cases social workers conducted second and third meetings but felt discouraged for other reasons. They obtained further clues about a person's circumstances and psychological make-up which influenced their subsequent decision that future association with him was likely to be unproductive. People's discursive accounts of previous difficulties had the effect of demonstrating that their current problems were not unusual and did not represent crises. Staff also sensed little prospect of being able to effect permanent change. The individual who gave the impression of having shopped indiscriminately for help and was confused over the social worker's role, enabled that practitioner to resolve any initial ambivalence about his obligation to intervene.

If a social worker came to a quick conclusion about some person's ineligibility he ran little risk of raising expectations, or at least less risk than if, from a client's point of view, a case began auspiciously because the worker seemed prepared to investigate matters at length. If such a start was not maintained people felt let down and discouraged. For example, following his first meeting with Mr Hay and with a view to impressing upon a charitable organization that the family merited financial help, the social worker had taken away this man's army-discharge papers. These contained the testimonial, 'hard working, diligent and accurate in all his work, always well turned out, polite, sober and trustworthy, popular with all ranks'. Mr Hay was pleased that the social worker seemed to think that such fulsome praise would impress others, including representatives of the charity, yet the two parties only ever met once again and virtually nothing happened in between. Not knowing why the social worker had lost interest, Mr Hay re-emphasized the deserving nature of his predicament in relation to that of others and thus maintained his own sense of self-respect and integrity. How such self-appraisal was influenced by the social worker's actions can be illustrated by tracing Mr Hay's interpretation of events, from his initial expectations of social work, his impressions following a first interview to his final explanation. Elaborating his initial assumptions,

A person that has worked hard all his life is not aware of these things.

I thought social work was for the down-and-outs.

Following their first meeting, Mr Hay gained the impression, not only by what was said but also by the army testimonials being taken away, that the social worker was both interested in and shared his points of view about his difficulties. In these circumstances his contention that he had always considered it shameful to be dependent on others, to have to ask for help, had been somewhat nullified.

With Mr B. it was different. He was a person prepared to listen to your views instead of just jumping in without giving you a chance to speak like I got from the others.

Later, when faced with the dilemma of having to explain why the social worker had not pursued the matter, his verdict was that what had happened proved that only the non-deserving, the criminals, the 'winos' could receive financial assistance and other forms of help from that source. This lifelong expectation, temporarily suspended on account of the treatment he had received following a first meeting, had now been confirmed.

What I've learnt is what I've always thought. Decent respectable people, they don't get help.

Concerning experiences of social work limited to such audition-type exchanges, three points can be made by way of summary. Firstly, such case management gave clients few clues about social workers' reasons for coordination or non-coordination of activities. Secondly, because the bases of decisions were not made explicit, clients were left guessing at the turn of events: some whose requests had not been met were confused about what had occurred yet remained uncritical; those who had been helped were not always sure why and wanted to express gratitude. Thirdly, clients who felt let down wanted to defend their own moral worth. They did so by emphasizing their belief that social workers were interested in helping the unworthy.

Sharing information

The management of middle-range cases was characterized by objectives and procedures familiar to and under the guidance of each worker, who considered it desirable practice to involve people in discussing the criteria on which to base decisions or their attempt to influence others'. In contrast to case management limited to audition-type exchanges, they did not want, and were not always able, to control the outcomes. They expected to mention to interviewees their reactions to their request and to share other information by recalling what had occurred in similar cases. Because such work involved reliance on some taken-for-granted knowledge of what to do and how to do it *and* referred to decisions seen by staff as having important consequences, the cases were popular and some enjoyed priority status. Although expecting their requests to be dealt with formally and in a meeting, people learned that this was not what the social worker had in mind and that it would be in their interests to cooperate. His objective was not merely to obtain information from first impressions but to check on these in the course of several meetings. However, the distinguishing feature of interaction was that the criteria on which decisions were based were usually negotiable and made known. Such exchanges included interviews with families requesting special accommodation for a disabled or handicapped member, with prospective adoptive parents and with those thinking of placing children for adoption.

Decision-making characterized by sharing of information occurred in two categories of cases: (i) those in which the social worker's objective was to make or recommend a decision that a client deserved some 'resource'; (ii) those in which the social worker was trying to ensure that the clients made a worthy decision. Interaction affecting workers' willingness and ability to share information can be illustrated with examples from each category.

Deserving some resource
Social workers' familiarity with certain objectives and means of implementing them involved having ideas about the approximate number of interviews needed to fulfil their task. This time assumption gave structure to case management. For example, a worker responsible for families with handicapped children had specialized in this work and when the information at allocation was that parents were requesting help with accommodation, she knew she would be following well-rehearsed steps of assessment. Experience had taught that family relationships and attitudes to chidren could not be foreseen, that such information could seldom be obtained quickly. Families' or their referral agents' requests for

day-care accommodation required investigation by interviewing parents and child and, if possible, introducing them to relevant residential staff. Information and impressions gathered during such meetings could substantiate the grounds of an application and how it compared with families with similar needs.

When people learned that the length of time to assess their needs was to be extended, they *could* manage their presentation of themselves and their request differently. Expecting future meetings enabled people to convey points of view on one occasion and elaborate them subsequently. For example, the father of a mentally retarded teenager had clarified during one meeting that if his wife did not get out of the house during the day she would break down from the strain of caring for their son. He had stressed that his son was one of the family, that their motives in asking for day-care accommodation were to help, not reject. On a second meeting grandparents were introduced and confirmed their son's contention about the purpose of his application. The social worker shared the family's interpretation, that they were not making their request, as had others in her opinion, 'as a form of escape'. She had been impressed by the grandparents' attitude and the whole family's 'sort of built-in cultural pattern of looking after their own'.

Encouraging families to be explicit about their hopes for help, and staff trying to be equally frank about factors affecting services, involved a process of negotiation which had risks. Expectations were raised, people changed their interpretations of what was desirable and possible. This happened with people who were taken on visits to sheltered accommodation for the aged and day-care centres for handicapped children. In a few instances, adults ultimately turned down vacancies saying they had changed their minds about their requirements. They had notions of what was good enough for them. What had been offered was not acceptable.

Discussions aimed at identifying criteria on which to base decisions were particularly characteristic of meetings with prospective adoptive parents. Such cases will be a familiar example of staff concern with assessing worth but are as germane an illustration of this thesis, that value judgements about people are at the hub of social workers' decisions, as are other negotiations in which this point is more easily camouflaged.

Prospective adoptive parents anticipated that aspects of their past and present circumstances would be investigated. They expected to be assessed, wondered what questions would be asked and had discussed with one another what credentials influenced the outcome of such applications. A husband who had been married previously and his wife, who had been the mother of a child whom she had placed for adoption, had discussed whether this past would disqualify their application. They were in their late 30s and wondered also whether this would count against them. They hoped that such an irrevocable piece of biography would be regarded by any interviewer as compensated by their being in good health and 'young in spirit'. Another couple reassured themselves that having only just reached the minimal age of 25 and being armed with medical evidence that they were unlikely to have their own children, must increase their chances of being passed. Both couples believed that their secure employment and income and their ownership of comfortable homes with at least one spare room would enhance their prospects. They expected social workers to ask for information about family background, age, health and income, but were not sure what other factors might be discussed. These applicants, who had some prior idea of the probable criteria affecting decisions, were highly motivated to cooperate even though informality was unexpected. They were initially agreeably surprised by the conversational, casual nature of their interviews.

A social worker's observation as to how interviews would be conducted was a first sign that interviewees' participation would affect assessment. Prospective adoptive parents gained the impression from first meetings that the interviewer wanted to obtain a picture of them by getting to know them informally, rather than by obtaining a profile from a completed questionnaire. Staff confirmed that this was the gist of what they had said and this had been their intention. They described this style of interviewing – stressed by one as a form of co-partnership – not as an attempt to disguise objectives but as a skilful way to obtain personal information. They regarded this task as involving several personal and probably interesting interviews. To informalize such exchanges one social worker tried to share her view of what was going on because,

> It's a process I would hate to go through myself, so I am quite sympathetic towards them. I usually try to reassure them.

Applicants sensed the interviewer's reactions and remembered others' advice about the progress of applications. For example, in between interviews with the social worker, one couple joined a discussion group with other prospective parents. They not only received notification of their suitability, the social worker having explained that she only suggested people should join a group if she planned to recommend them, but also learned some consensus views about desirable attributes of adoptive parents. They recalled that these group discussions centred on characteristics of model parents, of values and practices in child upbringing which it would be desirable to emulate; they had examined the importance of telling adopted children about their natural parents, when and how such information could be given.

Making a worthy decision

Social workers' assumptions about the desirability of people participating in, if not having control over, decisions affecting their future, reflected their attitudes towards types of cases as well as the idiosyncracies of people. Regarding work with mothers deliberating whether to keep a child or place him for adoption, concern with 'worthiness' had two meanings. Firstly, staff did not hesitate to intervene; unmarried mothers in general were worth all the costs of involvement. Secondly, social workers wanted to guide parents into making a 'worthy' decision.

Staff were very interested in this second objective but relatively powerless because the decision was not theirs. Yet they wanted to satisfy themselves over a parent's ability to care for her child by assessing the mother and those closely associated with her, usually relatives. However, assumptions that such work was important because it involved making a decision in the best interests of a child did not mean that staff should be openly interventionist. Aware that the ultimate decision rested with the mother, social workers interpreted their role as assessing under what circumstances and at what point they felt no further responsibility for the outcome. They had to manage the dilemma of wanting to reassure themselves that the right decision was made yet not being able to ensure it, of having a responsibility to obtain and give information yet avoid stating categorically what they thought the mother should do. This involved taking time and posing routine questions, conveying opinion about sound and sensible decisions, not by giving advice directly but by mentioning their experiences of what had occurred in other cases. They recalled girls who had 'made a mess of it' by keeping a baby but subsequently losing interest, regarding him as an obstacle to the freedom to go out to work, to have a social life. These prior considerations influenced impressions whether an unmarried mother's decision to keep a child was sensible and would be successful.

Unmarried mothers had had unpleasant experiences regarding

others' reaction to their marital status and some felt discredited in their own eyes. One girl had been so ashamed that she had not informed her family of her situation. The parents of another ostracized her, the father saying that she had brought disgrace to the family name and had ruined her life because no decent man would have her. Such reactions influenced the mothers' feelings about wanting to meet or talk to anyone at that time. The social workers, although wanting to be sympathetic, were also concerned to avoid giving the impression that they thought this should be a simple decision. They wanted the mothers to share their assumptions about the importance of taking time, that there were risks in making the 'wrong' decision, risks to the mother if she gave up a baby and regretted it, risks to the child's future if he was kept 'unrealistically'.

Giving information about adoption and the time span before any decision could be finalized was the most manageable and unambiguous feature of exchanges. Regarding placement of children for adoption, social workers also felt able to express their feelings openly, seldom being in a dilemma over supporting a parent's final decision to part with a child. However, depending on their reactions to the mother, decisions to keep a child were perceived variously. Although social workers stressed that ideally theirs was a neutral role, there were circumstances under which they wanted to be partisan. Two unmarried mothers' impressions were that the social worker was stressing the disadvantages of keeping a child. From each worker's point of view this strategy was influenced by *prima facie* evidence of a difficult future. A single girl, Susan, had no mother to support her and the social worker pointed out the advantages of the baby being adopted. However, the mothers' willingness to anticipate future difficulties as well as discuss present feelings, was regarded as evidence of a responsible attitude. If the mothers participated in discussions about possible handicaps in being unmarried, a social worker's pessimism about a baby's prospects changed, if not to optimism, at least to a feeling that there were grounds for supporting the mother's decision and limiting their own responsibility. Those who wanted to keep their baby but denied that future problems would arise and did not discuss long-term implications, such as marriage prospects, made it difficult for staff to be neutral.

Mothers recalled questions about a baby making future marriage unlikely and whether not being married would produce unsurmountable difficulties in bringing up a child. One social worker was reassured because a mother was likely to be married at some stage in the near future. However, from these mothers' points of view the marriage issue had been only one of several items discussed and had not been given undue attention. Marriage prospects were only one of a number of considerations influencing staff prognosis of a mother's ability to maintain her independence even with a baby. Other impressions were derived from information about the prospect of employment and about the reputation of a girl's circle of friends or advisers. For example, a single girl who had had a job and lived in a 'well organized flat' was considered sensible and capable of managing on her own. Another girl was seen as 'frail, physically and mentally . . . unrealistic about money or children' and unlikely to manage. Supporting evidence for these conclusions came from appraisal of the reliability of those who had influenced the girls into keeping their children. In the first case a father's and relations' promise of support had impressed. In the second, the girl had received advice from her peers in a mother-and-baby home and in the form of 'unrealistic pressure from a sister-in-law who was childless'. Such confidants were judged likely to have given advice for sentimental not practical considerations.

Disapproving of a decision to keep a child posed staff with a dilemma: to argue to themselves and colleagues that the decision was the mother's and their minimal responsibility in sharing useful information had been fulfilled; to redefine the mother's problem and their objective. This development could lead to case management with other characteristics. For example, a social worker thought that the girl who accepted the advice of friends in a mother-and-baby home to keep her child, would run into difficulties and want to reverse her decision later. She felt obliged to help the girl yet also give lukewarm 'support' for a decision she did not agree with. She kept the case open, invited the girl to make use of the agency and undertook to visit her in her lodgings. Such objectives involved not only the obligation to get and give information in a relatively systematic way, but also a relationship of closer liaison.

Interdependence and alliance

Some meetings were characterized quickly or ultimately by a sense of interdependence and alliance. Developments leading to such a relationship began with a social worker perceiving some condition meriting intervention: a crisis, someone having difficulties inconsistent with what he knew of this person's past and therefore 'out of character', or someone whose history represented a challenge. The social workers' ideological assumptions about the purpose and value of casework led to a different process of establishing worth than in those two interpersonal contexts discussed previously. Having established ground for intervention, subsequent exchanges involved trying to provide personal support as a test of that theory and belief that people could and should be helped to help themselves. Recipients confirmed the value of such help by reassuring that practitioner about the usefulness of his occupation, as in their willingness to cooperate in ways which showed they understood what he was trying to do. Such reciprocity and sense of equality in relationship confirmed the value of a worker's persistence in maintaining liaison. The processes contributing to such confirmation, not the duration of social work, were the distinguishing features of these exchanges.

Failure to confirm worth
Not in every case was a social worker's initial interest reinforced by an immediately favourable response, as when people welcomed the prospect of further meetings. Social workers' first impressions, though tentative, were in several cases strong enough to encourage them to carry out second and third meetings, almost in spite of clients' reactions. However, there came a point at which the social worker felt discouraged by resistance or denial that his intervention could be helpful. Such 'non-cooperation' occurred for a variety of reasons, including feelings of shame associated with contact with this outsider, because people regarded his style as off-putting and saw little to be gained from future meetings, because the social worker did not seem interested in the things which interested them or the worker's remedy seemed irrelevant in view of their changed circumstances.

From the social worker's point of view, initial commitments not being sustained were accounted for by people's failure to keep appointments or their being elusive to meet in other respects; by their diffidence or indifference or when one worker was succeeded by another and the new one did not share his predecessor's objectives. Faced with discouraging responses and in view of other and pressing commitments, staff lowered their sense of priority yet continued contact through occasional, brief and well spaced out visits, or lost interest altogether despite earlier consensus about problems.

At some point a social worker needed confirmation of his initial impressions of worthiness, the reassurance that he had been able to communicate his interest and convince someone that seeking his support was not only no trouble but was welcomed. Keeping appointments, participating in discussions about themselves, but not necessarily about any current problem, showing other evidence of being deserving as in the care of children, were grounds for making a further commitment of time, energy and other resources.

Establishing and confirming worth

Although a sense of mutual trust and interest was an idealized future casework goal, this quality of rapport sometimes dated from a first meeting. This happened in the case of a mother (Mrs Barter) referred by her doctor as being depressed. Sometimes this mutuality occurred only after several meetings, some reinterpretation of a problem and the provision of various forms of support. This happened with a Mrs Vera, who was not eligible for the nursery-school vacancy she had asked for but whose cold and poorly furnished home had suggested to the social worker that she and her family had other difficulties.[4]

Those traits and responses which forged alliances and produced that highly valued sense of interdependence can be highlighted by examining firstly, the criteria affecting the offer of loans and secondly, some mutual benefits in relationships. The exchanges focusing on these issues show each party's personal and professional sources of interest in establishing and confirming a sense of moral worth.

Loans were offered to some families not only because the social worker felt they needed such immediate help but also because, in his judgement, there seemed to be a good prospect of their being able to manage without outside help at some point in the future. Of 11 cases in which people said they hoped for some form of financial help, in only four did people receive some small and indirect cash help as in the payment of a bill, the offer of grocery and clothes vouchers. None of these 11 were offered loans. In three other cases, in which clients did not ask for money, loans of £20 and over were given. Such help went to those who did not ask for it directly. Initiatives leading to the offer of loans came from the social workers. They regarded the families as suffering financial difficulties caused partly by circumstances such as low wages, temporary unemployment and the desertion of a husband, which were beyond the control of the people concerned. Staff therefore felt that the families were deserving and had earned such aid. The notion 'having earned' was an important means of reassuring recipients that this was not charity, that they were not getting something for nothing. The 'depressed mother', Mrs Barter, needed encouragement to disengage from what she saw as the shame associated with such an offer. She explained that following a second meeting with the social worker:

> She gave me money as a loan. At first I thought, it's worse than welfare, the next best thing is I'll be queueing up at a soup kitchen. But she explained about it and at the time I found it helpful. . . .

Loans were a means to an end. Giving such money was an opportunity to elaborate that ideally social work was a shared task which involved helping people to help themselves. The social worker selected people likely to benefit from such an exercise and did so on certain grounds. Mrs Barter was 'uncharacteristically' in financial difficulties. The Vera family who received a loan of £20 were seen as 'secure emotionally, depending on the children a lot, mutually reinforcing each other'. They were also regarded as motivated, making an effort, 'there was something there which we could work with positively'. On these grounds some financial aid could be justified, as it had to be in explanations to seniors, as part of a long-term strategy. Not only recipients were concerned about the moral implications of such gestures. Social workers were also at pains to stress that although this was a loan, they hoped it would not obscure more important features of relationships. They were not rent collectors, neither were subsequent meetings to be used as an opportunity to check on repayments. To resolve this role conflict, debt collector versus family counsellor, agent of control versus supporter of change, staff asked recipients to pay the money to the central office rather than directly to them and attached no strict conditions of repayment, a practice which appeared to be nationwide. (Newman 1974; SWSG 1973).

Loans symbolized that people were valued and, as in similar gift relationships, were a powerful force binding people together (Schwartz 1967; Titmuss 1970). However, the professionals did not regard this instrument as central to the identity of their function in this context and were successful in getting their message across. The Vera family explained that they realized their social worker was different from and had nothing to do with housing officials, that he wasn't just concerned about rent arrears. They accepted that he wanted to get to know them, to piece together information about their background and in these respects should be counted a friend. This interpretation was reinforced not only by the loan but because, in the father's eyes, the social worker's reasons for giving financial help showed that he understood the true cause of their difficulties. The family had earned such help because they were trying to bring up small children on unrealistically low wages.

Enabling people to articulate some sense of relationship and feelings of compatibility expressed the attainment of a cherished professional goal. Sometimes this was achieved quickly. In other cases it was the return on a more elaborate and time-consuming investment. The willingness to listen, empathize, keep commitments, make contact with others on a client's behalf and provide support through friendship, had paid off. People began to take for granted the social worker's positive interest and attitude. The worker regarded such involvement as little trouble and expected to meet informally, as far as possible on equal terms.

Mrs Barter, the deserted mother who had received a loan, reflected at the end of six months on some characteristics of helpfulness, the young worker's relaxed informality as evidenced by her discussing spontaneously several topics.

> [With her] you can have a smoke and sit and chat. . . . It's been nice to have somebody to talk to who can actually solve problems through. She's more like a friend and yet at the same time she's concerned as to how you are actually managing. But it doesn't give you the same feeling at all.

Mrs Barter had enabled the social worker to practice in the way which had influenced her choice of occupation. She had transferred from nursing because that job had given her neither autonomy, the time or encouragement to respond to someone as a whole person, nor the opportunity to anticipate social and psychological conditions associated with illness. Of her relationship with Mrs Barter,

> It's unusual to find somebody who is able to make use of our skills. A lot of people are unable to do this but Mrs Barter is an articulate person.

Association with Mrs B. enabled this social worker to distinguish her role from others in social work and her job in general from that of other occupations. Mrs B. reciprocated the social worker's feelings, emphasizing that at least in this person's company she no longer felt either so depressed, deserted or undeserving. Such a relationship altered her view of her own moral worth. She recalled feeling guilty and depressed over the break-up of her marriage[5] and added:

> When I was depressed she was more or less somebody like a chum . . . if somebody like her is going to bother to come it gives you a feeling that you are not on your own because round here the

neighbours are all old or else they are out working. You never hear or see a soul.

Compatibility resembled co-partnership when people enabled the worker to be and feel helpful. One social worker explained why a disabled woman's temporary dependence on her had been rewarding.

> She is rewarding to work with because she's not over-dependent and yet she likes to be a little dependent which is nice. Also I find she communicates easily which makes it far easier for me anyway. And she's the sort of person I find it quite easy to establish a meaningful relationship with.

From the old lady's point of view the 'meaningful relationship' occurred because she identified in this worker some valued attribute of herself and reciprocity was ensured. She expressed gratitude for blankets and money for a special diet, but added:

> I've found she's a bit like myself, she has a good understanding of human nature.

Some relationship of interdependence was a resource for the client because it acted as an incentive for the worker to continue to believe that the cost of such involvement was worthwhile. This was important for a profession which was receiving national publicity for failures but finding it difficult to identify let alone measure successes and received scant feedback about them. From clients' points of view, compatibility involved having confidence in someone with whom they could discuss several topics, because that person showed consistent interest in their affairs and knew of ancillary services, income maintenance or the availability of domestic help.[6] The appearance of competence helped construct a view of a credible, helpful person. However, these features of face-to-face exchanges do not explain entirely commitments made in spite of other work and other cases. What at first sight appeared to represent only the fit of 'suitability', or personal compatibility, can on closer inspection be seen to be related to organizational considerations and in particular to staff ideologies. Only certain people and problems facilitated relationships in which the respondents were grateful for an opportunity to unburden themselves through discussion with someone they liked and trusted; a relationship which had characteristics of what psychiatrists like to refer to as a 'therapeutic alliance'.

Wanting and being able to sense compatibility in relationships reinforced a social worker's initial interpretation of the kind of people these were and the task he should fulfil. On the other hand, if he felt only unease in people's company – as with the woman

described as being almost impossible to have a conversation with
– this compounded that person's lack of other resources.
Compatibility encouraged the worker, was a form of leverage for
clients and confirmation of a sense of self-respect for both. In this
context they were thrown together as fellow citizens with a
common concern. By interpreting the roles of helper and helped in
ways which were acceptable to both, each enabled the other to
forget, at least temporarily, any unworthy or less worthy aspects of
predicament and profession. These clients had not expected such a
personal social service to be among the range of central or local
government provisions. The social worker had been able to offer
'solutions' not only because they were within his sphere of
competence but also because they were among the tasks which gave
greatest job satisfaction. Some ideal professional image had been
proved capable of being fulfilled.

Summary

Although, initially at least, clients knew little of the criteria
affecting decision-making in social-work agencies, there was
congruence between their anxieties and beliefs and the
considerations which influenced social workers' management of
their tasks. Both groups were concerned with certain values as
illustrated by clients' attitudes to maintaining their independence,
social workers welcoming some forms of dependence but not
others, both groups' distinctions between deserving, less deserving
and non-deserving people and situations, assessment of the costs
of giving and receiving help, the costs to layman and professional
of being involved with one another. This congruence was part of
their shared historical legacy, part of a continuing dilemma and
debate about State responsibility in meeting the needs of
dependent groups, and the means and consequences of doing so.[7]
The social workers' ideologies enabled them to manage this
responsibility to clients and give attention to their own concerns
with occupational identity and job satisfaction. The clients had to
manage not only their several material or other personal
difficulties but also some sense of powerlessness in the face of
officialdom and, in most cases, feelings of stigma associated with
their involvement with the social-work agencies.
  The similar concerns of client and social worker emerged in
their meetings and were capable of being resolved there, at least
temporarily. But in audition-type exchanges client participation

was minimal. In conducting other interviews the social workers followed procedures for sharing information about the bases of their decisions. A third type of case management involved relationships of interdependence which included some reciprocity of feelings between clients and social workers and tacit acknowledgement of shared goals.

In each of these different contexts of social worker/client meetings, both parties were concerned about identity, about the roles of helper and helped. Both were involved in some competition for allegedly scarce resources, both competing to help and for help. Even though most clients were deferential to people in positions of authority, they were not without means of influencing social workers. Some, albeit unwittingly, enabled a practitioner to bolster beliefs about the useful purpose, the worthy character of his job. An incentive for a social worker was a form of leverage for a client. Some clients and staff were concerned to show that only people traditionally regarded by others as not worth troubling about merited attention: the social worker who saw the 'hopeless' ex-prisoner as a challenge; the client whose experience of being let down confirmed his views that only the unworthy received social-work help.

In managing any one case the social worker was working out that occupational dilemma of being officially committed to helping all who were allocated as cases yet conscious of the possibility of supporting only some. The grounds for deciding that some people deserved help, that others should be supported in their decisions, were not always immediately clear to staff. They often had responsibility for cases in which they felt there were few guidelines and scant resources. Some clients appeared to have only hazy notions of what was wrong, what they wanted or what they needed and were uncertain of agency functions. These were the immediate conditions contributing to decisions being based on judgements of 'moral character', an assessment of people and their problems *in relation to* a worker's assumption about the importance of general categories of work, what he felt he could do in a particular case and what he felt he was expected to do by others. Value judgements concerning the unworthy or worthy character of a type of case in general in relation to an individual in particular became criteria for decisions about the help people needed and the action a social worker should take. This usually involved each social worker in avoiding situations of greatest uncertainty in which the steps to follow were not well known, in which he felt powerless to help, in which continued association held out little prospect of change. It did involve making commitments to work with people in contexts of less uncertainty, in which there were known procedures, or there seemed some prospect of change, as when clients reciprocated a social worker's interest by evidence of their being willing and able to help themselves.

NOTES

1 See the discussion in the earlier reference to this case in Chapter 4, p. 65 f.
2 A reference to the social worker contacting electricity and gas boards regarding her arrears and his obtaining a second-hand television set 'to combat her loneliness.'
3 See the reference in Chapter 1, p. 4.
4 Others who were never seen in their homes were, therefore, handicapped in conveying any impression of their living conditions.
5 See Chapter 4, pp. 93–4.
6 In cases requiring legal knowledge of housing rights and husband/wife disputes over children, some people were disappointed when a social worker did not have such information and could at best only promise to find out. This 'finding out' was not always immediately reassuring to people who hoped for a quick answer to an issue which had been a source of anxiety for a long time.
7 Although the following parallel between past attitudes to the operation of the Poor Law and some social workers' present dislikes in their occupation is tenuous, there is indication that theirs' and clients' concern about moral worth had links not just to the immediate past. Pinker argues that in nineteenth-century Britain the final humiliation for the aged poor was the prospect of a pauper's funeral. In the local authority agency in the mid 1970s the 'most avoided task', because it was regarded as 'not really social work' was the responsibility for making arrangements for the burial of the destitute, a job left to an ex-welfare officer who 'did not mind' such tasks. See Pinker, (1971), p. 78.

Chapter 6

Issues and Innovations

The meaning of social work derived from the clients' and the social workers' perspectives on their face-to-face meetings makes some of the dominant themes in the official literature look a little tarnished. For example, the goal of rationalizing services by avoiding overlap between departments' responsibilities has been followed by the development of new priorities and new demarcation disputes between social workers, and between social workers and other agencies. The effect of increasing publicity about the public's entitlements to services provided by social workers is lessened by many clients' and potential clients' continued confusion about social workers' functions and the feelings of stigma which they associate with the business of seeking help from others. Some policy makers' hopes that social workers might use their discretionary powers to promote social change have to be judged against a picture of social work which resembles some of society's existing arrangements for maintaining social order and control. For example, the clients' and the social workers' use of value judgements to assess their own and others' needs mirrors a stratified society which expects groups of people to merit certain kinds of services according to their individual achievements and personal life styles, and which takes for granted the importance of distinguishing between the deserving and the non-deserving, the worthy and the unworthy.

Social work alone cannot be expected to eliminate those forces which maintain class divisions and other forms of discrimination between different groups of needy people. It could alter people's expectations of people in positions of authority, the arrangements for the delivery of personal social services and the kinds of relationships that exist between help seekers and help givers. To achieve even these goals would require social administrators, social-work educators and various agencies' different social-work staff to tackle some of the issues in the present operation of social work. The issues identified in this study concern the effect of social workers' ideologies on their organization of their work and their interpretations of clients' problems; the powerlessness of clients in the context of certain types of case management; the moral calculations which affected clients' decisions to seek help, their presentations of their requests and social workers' decisions about the grounds for their own intervention in any one case.

The social workers' ideology of casework influenced them into identifying certain tasks as prestigious and ones which they would enjoy spending time on. This lessened the value of work with clients whose problems and reactions to them could not be defined in casework terms. Faced with people who had imprecise knowledge of social work and were inexperienced in the business of bargaining with any professionals, social workers could decide how much information they wanted and how much information they would provide. Only where they felt that the means and ends of their relationships with clients should be characterized by some sense of interdependence were they sensitive to their ability to control the outcome of meetings. However, they may not always have been immediately conscious of the considerations affecting their continued intervention. For example, the extent to which a referral agent's motives in sending someone to a social worker were considered as indicating the genuineness of a client's request affected most staff's deliberations about how to use their time. Some clients' relatives were regarded as having influenced the clients into trying to get something for nothing. Some professional outsiders, such as hospital paediatricians, were regarded as unlikely to have made a referral unless child and parents had a serious difficulty meriting immediate attention. The connotation of a referral agent's behaviour was usually referred to at allocation meetings. It was seldom explicitly acknowledged as having influenced a social worker's subsequent management of a case or his assumptions about available resources. 'Resources' did not refer to a closely prescribed and fixed quantity of personnel, facilities or cash. The discovery of resources, as in finding vacancies in day-care centres, the creation of resources, as in working out with some individual how they might plan their future social activities, depended on social workers perceiving tasks which were ideologically palatable. As interpreters and intermediaries all social workers have the power to make links between their agency responsibilities and an individual's needs. Regarding this task they should always be trying to answer the question which I have asked elsewhere. 'Does the familiar plea "lack of resources" reflect an identifiable lack of personnel and plant or a decision that some people cannot be helped in terms of how a social worker, immediate colleagues and others construe some ideal functions of social work, those aspects of practice defined routinely as high priority?' (Rees 1976).

Publicity has often been focused on some misuse of power by other state employees, as when police fabricate evidence, when some prospective immigrants are refused entry, when 'undesirables' are deported, when prison sentences seem unrealistically harsh. Social workers' case management has only been subject to similar scrutiny when some sensation occurs, as when staff in one part of the country are alleged to have ignored legal regulations in admitting patients to psychiatric hospitals (Bowder 1977) or when social workers appear to have overlooked their responsibility to visit children who were in physical or moral danger. Yet social workers are part of an army of welfare-state representatives who have the potential to affect daily the lives of large numbers of people through their handling of cases. Their use of such power through the operation of their ideologies requires constant review. (See Goldberg and Fruin 1976.)

Social workers' skills should include the ability to uncover and weigh the significance of events in the wider context of the clients' world. This requires the imagination to develop questions and the flair to encourage people to talk about the events which led to their coming to an agency. But agency information about the clients' world could be compiled more systematically if representatives of clients, ex-clients and other referral agents acted as special resource groups to social workers. In this capacity they could enable social workers, seniors and other managers included, to learn about and perhaps change some local factors affecting people's use of services. The apparently casual behaviour of some sources of referral compounded clients' existing handicaps in having only imprecise knowledge of agencies' functions. Some referral agents did not know much about social work. Some did not want to know. Some apparently wanted some people, whom they regarded as troublesome, out of their way as soon as possible. Some referral agents contributed to clients' sense of shame and confusion by referring them without their knowledge or permission.

In this study some social workers observed that although the number of old people loomed large in their and their colleagues' caseloads, close involvement with the aged was avoided because it was regarded as not the best use of a social worker's time. Helping people who had material difficulties was also not highly valued. This was expected to be unrewarding work: no special techniques were required; permanent improvements in these people's lives were unlikely; some poor people had been known to be ungrateful. If these social workers had had a responsibility to consult regularly with client groups, they might have developed ideologies leading to the reallocation of priorities and the consequent development of resources to meet these groups' needs. At least they might have halted the momentum of some traditional agency specializations.

Regular consultation between professional employees and representatives of client groups, such as claimants' unions, psychiatric patients, prisoners' wives and single parents, could lessen the sense of distance between clients and agencies. Some clients' inclusion in specialist team meetings could de-mystify their impressions of what social work is about and improve professional/public relationships. In discussing the usefulness of including clients' perspectives in agency evaluation, Giordano goes even further and suggests that such consultation with clients parallels the success of including industrial workers in decision-making processes, thus contributing to better employee morale, decreased turnover and absenteeism and greater work satisfaction (Giordano 1977).

Client groups' involvement in agency or area-team planning meetings would put into effect social workers' beliefs about the value of casework, namely that a most important goal in social work is not so much doing things for people as enabling them to help themselves. Such public participation is not the preserve only of community development projects. The experience of being consulted enables clients to revise their expectations of what it is like to be a client, to see themselves according to what they are able to do rather than in the light of what they have done to them. For example, some recipients of welfare benefits in Ontario have explained that they would value taking part in agency policy meetings because this would enable them to make constructive suggestions for improvements in services and not just complaints (Rees and Atkison 1978).

Some critics will no doubt point out that client representatives' participation in meetings with social workers would result in their being co-opted. Their views would not be taken seriously or would be absorbed in the professionals' existing practices. It is worth testing whether this would be one of the developments arising from such regular client consultation.

The numerous educational institutions which benefit from providing professional training for social workers also have a responsibility to familiarize their students with the realities of the clients' world. To do otherwise is to disregard clients' and potential clients' interests. I doubt whether this development occurs. On the contrary, social-work educators' concern with unravelling 'methods of intervention' seems similar to psychiatrists' interests in proliferating therapies. These therapies, says Bitensky, are produced by professionals for professional audiences and are so quickly replaced that there is little time to assess whether they have any bearing on patients' lives or are effective in other ways in treating mental illness. Before the public knows of or can express its disenchantment with the latest fad a new nostrum is introduced to guide the perplexed (Bitensky 1976). If social-work students and social workers concentrate on mastering the techniques of methods, they will also be able to shelter behind them and so dodge the issues surrounding occupational ideologies and the destructive conditions in some clients' lives.

The theories underlying social workers' methods of intervention can only be elaborated and substantiated if they have an empirical as well as a philosophical base. This emphasis on empiricism – a testing-out through purposeful observation and documentation of the meaning to clients and professionals of their separate concerns and of their interaction – does not preclude teachers and practitioners from developing theories or from taking ideological stands. It does admonish them to identify the conditions affecting any new approach and to answer the questions: what information is taken for granted by the participants, how are resources defined, what values affect interaction and what criteria are used to evaluate outcomes? A detailed appraisal of 'perspectives in social work' has provided a baseline for analysing the practice of social work according to the findings of different kinds of research (Timms and Timms 1977).

An empirical as well as a philosophical approach to understanding clients' and social workers' behaviour would highlight the conditions affecting the provision of personal services. Such an approach would also make social-work training potentially a lot more innovative, certainly a lot more interesting for students than if concepts such as 'seeking help' and 'treatment' continue to be used uncritically. My documentation of clients' experiences shows that any image that social work involves people seeking help and receiving treatment is at best over-simplified, at worst thoroughly misleading. The 60 clients' pathways to social workers resembled the attempts of any new arrival in an unfamiliar city to discover the geographical location of important agencies, something about their official functions and their actual reputations in their dealings with the public. Lost at first, the newcomer eventually finds some bearings. At that point he may resign himself to managing through his own resourcefulness. If he persists he discovers later that although most officials are friendly not all are interested. Not every 'welfare man' will take seriously an enquirer's problems let alone be able to provide an immediate solution.

The concept 'treatment' can be robbed of its pretentiousness if the activities which are gathered under this label are defined. This involves analysing the effect of outside forces on client/social worker relationships. For example, the 38 social workers' sense of moral obligation towards only certain people and problems reflected their familiarity with work routines, and their assumptions about the most desirable attributes of their occupation. Each social worker spent some time in meetings with clients but also worked in association with administrators, committees and other professionals who gave him work and influenced potential clients' interpretations of his task. The social workers' ideologies incorporated the views of these others, in particular regarding the function of social work in a society in which respect for independence is highly valued. The clients also thought about these issues. They hoped that their views of their own moral worthiness would be shared by the social workers and result in their being passed as suitable for some resource or service. Even if their expectations of help were precise, they still made sense of social work through recollections of encounters with all sorts of people in positions of authority, the attitudes and advice of relations and acquaintances and other everyday pressures and preoccupations. In first exchanges and subsequently, the clients were usually in a less powerful position than the social workers. This happened partly because each social worker interpreted people's problems in such a way as to maintain a sense of coherence in and control over his work. It happened also because, notwithstanding official policy emphasis on universal access to services, admitting to some state of dependency was regarded by many clients as a sign of weakness or as too much trouble.

The clients' experiences of social work varied, not merely according to whether they felt they had been helped[1] but also from one interpersonal context to another, from brief audition-type interviews to relationships characterized by some sense of interdependence and alliance. As a result of such meetings some individuals' expectations of social work were confounded, their anxieties alleviated. They became favourable interpreters and often advocates of social work or the social worker, able to distinguish him or her as a person and that occupation in general in ways which matched staff explanations. Others' experiences confirmed their pessimistic views of all 'welfare services'. Although most were uncritical, they continued to regard an agency's functions as just part of an impersonal alliance of mostly anonymous officials. These interpretations did not match the social workers' accounts of their everyday tasks, let alone their ideals.

The meaning of social work conveyed by the clients' evaluations is far more important than knowing that a certain percentage were helped and an almost equally large number were not. The trouble with this sort of distinction is that it can perpetuate oversimplified impressions of what occurs between social workers and their clients. The practice of social work is seldom simple. (It is still worthwhile even if it is). It is often complex. Social workers have different ideologies and different styles in implementing them. Clients have different emotional reactions to apparently similar problems and different orientations to seeking help. The dissemination of information about the different forms of communication in client/social worker exchanges and about other activities contributing to clients being helped or not, is a prerequisite to building theories about processes of decision making in areas in which social workers have discretionary powers.

Some social work was complex because of clients' several entrenched difficulties. Other practice was complex because administrative routines and professional traditions hampered social workers' initial good intentions. This underlines the importance of experimenting with new forms of organization to meet people's needs. Agencies which are run through hierarchies and which are based on assumptions about professional/client roles are not flexible enough to respond to variations in the nature and extent of public demand. They don't always make the best use of their staff's different interests and skills. Through more open government in their agencies social workers could take initiatives to debureaucratize their own and other institutions. They should value unmasking the ideological bases of their decisions as much as they have valued the skill in encouraging clients to be frank about their problems. Such experiments could provide social workers and those academics involved in their training with a greater sense of relevance and satisfaction from their jobs. Such openness could improve clients' access to services and enable them to use agencies to find more satisfaction in their lives.

NOTE

1 Only a little over half of the clients said they had been helped. See Chapter 5.

Appendix

Sources of Information

Information was collected from social workers' and agency records, from informal discussions with social workers, clients and their families, housing visitors, supplementary-benefits officers, doctors and a lawyer. Meetings were attended in both agencies, including those to watch allocation procedures and explain the purpose of the research. Most meetings were planned, some occurred by chance. Most documents were asked for. Some, such as a senior administrator's speech explaining his department's policy regarding giving money, were unanticipated but fell like manna into the grateful researcher's lap. The main sources of information were clients' and social workers' tape-recorded accounts of their meetings. When a new case was allocated to a social worker who had agreed to take part in the research[1] he explained the researcher's interest and if the client agreed to be seen, the necessary information was passed to the researcher. Interviews with clients and their respective social workers took place in the former's home and the latter's office within one week of their first meeting and again on at least a second occasion four to six months later.

Collection of the sample began with 10 cases in which the researcher acted as observer and got to know families and social workers well for periods up to one year. This intensive study of a small number of cases provided not only some discoveries by inadvertency but also ideas which could be tested in the semi-structured interviewing of the larger sample of 50. The early and exploratory contacts provided insights from which questions were compiled for use in semi-structured interviews.

Not all clients' problems were discrete and any recording of difficulties depended upon the researcher's interpretations of things which people mentioned during the first research interview. An inventory in 60 cases was derived from six problem areas: financial (where the client had debts and could not manage); unemployment; sickness or disability; interpersonal (included clients' references to control of children and/or evidence of family break-up); housing (such as overcrowding); legal (such as requests for legal aid regarding civil actions over the custody of children). Taking the family as the unit for comparison, the incidence of problems was as follows: (Table A.1)

Table A.1 Problems in Specified Areas

Problem area	Financial	Unemploy- ment	Sickness/ disability	Inter- personal	Accom- modation	Legal
Times recorded in 60 cases	34	14	36	41	21	14

Another way of looking at these figures is to examine the number of problem areas associated with each case (Table A.2)

Table A.2 Problem areas in each case

No. of problem areas	No. of cases	Percentage
One	11	19
Two	21	35
Three	14	23
Four	8	13
Five	3	5
Six	3	5
Total	60	100

From Table A.2 it can be seen that 28 (46 per cent) of the sample showed evidence of three or more problem areas but a single problem was recorded for only 11 (19 per cent) of cases. The tables are reproduced as a reminder that the researcher's recording of events at one point in time would not necessarily be a guide to what followed. A social problem attributed by some outsider would not necessarily reflect a difficulty about which someone would complain or seek a solution from others. The recorded problems were not always conversation topics between client and social worker. They were involved in their own meetings and were asked to define situations for themselves.

The above assumptions set the project in a particular direction. They influenced the choice of interview questions, the collection of information, the selection of quotes throughout and of case studies in Chapter 4. The author was also involved in 'defining the situation'. For example, some cases were dropped from the sample when it seemed as though the further intervention of some outsider such as a social worker should take precedence over continued research.[2] Involvement with others no doubt affected the behaviour being studied. For example, some staff probably modified their objectives, at least verbally, because they were asked to be explicit about them. Some people asked questions as though the interviewers were social workers. Some information was given, some requests were refused; yet other developments, such as raising expectations of continued friendship were inevitable. They illustrate a dilemma of repeated interviewing.

'Canons of research demand that (the researcher) operate somewhat like a computer with all the appearances of a fellow human being' (Cicourel 1970). The effects of involvement with interviewees were recorded as part of the research, built into the analysis and regarded as data not bias.

NOTES

1 Of the social workers asked to participate in the project only two refused.
2 When a father was about to be sent to prison the interviewer took the family to see the social worker. This happened at the end of the research and the case was retained in the sample. Two other cases involving the failing health of isolated old people were referred back to the agencies and dropped from the sample.

References

Abstracts of Statistics, 1960–1975: London: HMSO.

Adams, P. and McDonald, N. 1968: Clinical cooling out of poor people, *American Journal of Orthopsychiatry* 38 (3), 457–63.

Arrow, K. 1963: Uncertainty and the welfare economics of medical care. *American Economic Review* LIII (5).

Balint, M. 1963: *The doctor, his patient and the illness*. London: Pitman.

Ball, D. W. 1970: 'The problematics of respectability. In Douglas, J. D., editor, *Deviance and respectability*. New York: Basic Books, 326–71.

Beck, B. 1967: Welfare as a moral category, *Social Problems* 14, 259–277.

Becker, H. S. 1963: *Outsiders*. New York: Free Press.

Bitensky, R. 1976: Tumult in therapyland. *Diogenes* 94, 110–120.

Blaxter, M. 1976: *The meaning of disability*. London: Heinemann.

Bowder, B. 1977: An act of abuse. *Community Care*, 10 August, 11–13.

Briar S. and Piliavin, I. 1964: Police encounters with juveniles. *American Journal of Sociology* LXXX (2), 206–14.

British Association of Social Workers. 1977: *The social work task*. Birmingham: BASW.

Carlen, P. 1976: *Magistrates' justice*. London: Martin Robertson.

Carmichael, C. 1969: Development in Scottish social work: changes in the law and implications for the future. *Applied Social Studies* 1 (1).

— 1977: Switch on the light. *New Society* 39 (746), 20 January.

Central Statistical Office, 1974: *Social Trends* No. 5. London: HMSO.

— 1976: *Social Trends* No. 7. London: HMSO.

Cicourel, A. 1970: *Method and measurement in sociology*. New York: Free Press.

Clarke, B. 1960: The 'cooling out' function in higher education. *American Journal of Sociology* 65, 569–76.

Clifford, D. 1975: Stigma and perception of social security services. *Policy and Politics* 3 (3).

Cloward, R. and Piven, F. 1976: Notes toward a radical social work. In Bailey, R. and Brake, M., editors, *Radical Social Work*. New York: Pantheon Books, vii–xviii.

Emerson, R. M. 1969: *Judging delinquents*. Chicago: Aldine.

Erikson, E. H. 1968: *Identity, youth and crisis*. New York: Norton.

Finer Committee, 1974: *Report of the committee on one-parent families*. London: HMSO, Cmnd. 5629.

Fischer, J. 1973: Is casework effective? *Social Work* 18 (1), 5–20.

Geertz, C. 1964: Ideology as a cultural system. In Apter, D., editor, *Ideology and discontent*. New York: Free Press, 56–64.

Giordano, P. 1977: The client's perspective in agency evaluation. *Social Work* 22 (1), 34–9.

Glampson, A. and Goldberg, E. 1976: Post Seebohm social services: (2) the consumer's viewpoint. *Social Work Today* 8 (6), 7–12.

Glampson, A., Glastonbury, B. and Fruin, D. 1977: Knowledge and perceptions of the social services. *Journal of Social Policy* 6 (1), 1–16.

Glastonbury, B., Burdett, M. and Austin, R. 1973: Community perceptions and the personal social services. *Policy and Politics* 1 (3).

Goffman, E. 1952: Cooling the mark out: some aspects of adaptations to failure. *Psychiatry* 15, 451–63.

— 1968: *Stigma*. Harmondsworth: Penguin.

— 1971: *The presentation of self in everyday life*. London: Penguin, 72.

Goldberg, E. M. and Neill, J. E. 1972: *Social work in general practice*. London: Allen and Unwin.

Goldberg, E. M. and Fruin, D. J. 1976: Towards accountability in social work. *The British Journal of Social Work* 6 (1), 3–22.

Hall, A. 1974: *The point of entry*. London: Allen and Unwin.

Hansard, 1970: *The parliamentary debates*, Vol. 310. 4 May to 29 May.

Hansen, D. A. 1969: Toward a theory of co-ordination in counselling and psychotherapy. In Hansen, D. A., editor, *Exploration in Sociology and Counselling*. Boston: Houghton Mifflin.

Horan, P. M. and Austin, P. L. 1974: The social bases of welfare stigma. *Social Problems* 21 (5), 648–57.

Jackson, B. and Marsden, D. 1972: *Education and the working class*. Harmondsworth: Penguin.

Jacobs, S. 1975: Rehousing in Glasgow: reform through community action. In Jones D., and Mayo, M., editors, *Community Work 2*. London: Routledge and Kegan Paul.

Jordan, B. and Moore, P. 1976: Whose concern? Squandering the rights of the aged. *Social Work Today* 6 (24).

Knightley, P. 1975: Should India be left to die? *Sunday Times*, 26 January.

Levinson, P. 1964: Chronic dependency: a conceptual analysis. *Social Service Review* 38 (4).

McKay, A., Goldberg, E. M. and Fruin, D. J. 1973: Consumers and a social services department. *Social Work Today* 4 (16).

McKinlay, J. B. 1974: Clients and organizations. In McKinlay, J. B., editor, *Processing people: cases in organizational behaviour*. London: Holt, Rinehart and Winston.

Mayer, J. E. and Timms, N. 1970: *The client speaks*. London: Routledge and Kegan Paul.

Meacher, M. 1973: *Rate rebates: a study of the effectiveness of means tests*. Poverty Research Series. London: CPAG.

Neill, J. E., Fruin, D., Goldberg, E. M. and Warburton, R. W. 1973: Reactions to integration. *Social Work Today* 4 (15), 458–65.

Neill, J., Warburton, W. and McGuiness, B. 1976: Post-Seebohm social services: the social worker's viewpoint. *Social Work Today* 8 (5), 9–14.

Newman, N., editor. 1974: *In cash or in kind – the place of financial assistance in social work*. Edinburgh: University Department of Social Administration.

Parker, R. 1967: Social administration and scarcity – the problem of rationing. *Social Work (UK)* 24 (2), 9–14.

Parsloe, P., Warren, E. and Gauldie, J. 1976: Social work as taught, *New Society*, 4 March.

Pearson, G. 1973: Social work as the privatized solution to public ills. *British Journal of Social Work* 3 (2), 209–23.

Phillips, D. L. 1963: Rejection, a possible consequence of seeking help for mental disorders. *American Sociological Review* XXIX, 963–72.

Pinker, R. 1971: *Social theory and social policy*. London: Heinemann.

— 1974: *Dependency and welfare*. Report to the Social Science Research Council.

Ragg, N. 1977: *People not cases*. London: Routledge and Kegan Paul.

Rees, S. J. 1974: No more than contact: an outcome of social work. *The British Journal of Social Work* 4 (3).

— 1976: Defining moral worthiness: grounds for intervention in social work. *Social Work Today* 7 (7), 203–6.

Rees, S. J. and Atkison, B. 1978: Perceptions of social work in Ontario. Unpublished paper. Wilfrid Laurier University, Waterloo, Ontario.

Reid, W. J. and Epstein, L. 1972: *Task-centred casework*. New York: Columbia University Press.

Richan, W. and Mendelsohn, A. 1973: *Social work the unloved profession*. New York. New Viewpoints.

Rose, H. 1973: Who can delabel the claimant? *Social Work Today* 4 (13), 409–13.

Roth, J. 1962: The treatment of tuberculosis as a bargaining process. In Rose, A., editor, *Human behaviour and social process*. London: Routledge and Kegan Paul.

Ryan, W. 1972: *Blaming the victim*. New York: Vintage Books.

Sachs, H. 1972: Notes on police assessment of moral character. In Sudnow, D., editor, *Studies in social interaction*. New York: Free Press, 280–93.

Sainsbury, E. 1975: *Social work with families*. London: Routledge and Kegan Paul.

Schutz, A. 1962: *Collected papers 1*. The problem of social reality. The Hague: Martinas Nijhoff.

Schwartz, B. 1967: The social psychology of the gift. *American Journal of Sociology* 73 (1).

Schwartz, S. H. 1970: Moral decision making and behaviour. In Macaulay, J. and Berkowitz, L., editors, *Altruism and helping behaviour*. New York: Academic Press.

Scott, R. A. 1969: *The making of blind men*. New York: Russell Sage, p. 77.

Scottish Office. 1966: *Social work and the community*, Edinburgh: HMSO, Cmnd. 3065.

Seebohm Committee 1968: *Local authority and allied personal social services*. London: HMSO.

Smith, G. and Harris, R. 1972: Ideologies of need and the organization of social work departments. *British Journal of Social Work* 2 (1).

Social Work Services Group (SWSG) 1968: Circular No. SW6. Edinburgh: HMSO.

— 1973: Scottish Social Work Statistics. Edinburgh: HMSO.

— 1974: Scottish Social Work Statistics. Edinburgh: HMSO.

Stanton, E. 1970: *Clients come last*. Beverly Hills: Sage.

Stevenson, O. 1977: Focus on the task of the local authority social worker. *Social Work Today* 9 (4).

Stimson, G. 1974: Obeying doctor's orders: a view from the other side. *Social Science and Medicine* 8, 97–104.

Strauss, A., Schutzman, L., Bucher, R., Ehrlich, D. and Sabshin, M. 1964: Psychiatric ideologies and psychiatric hospitals. In Strauss, A. *et al.*, *Psychiatric institutions and ideologies*. New York: Free Press.

Sudnow, D. 1967: *Passing on: the social organization of dying*. New York: Prentice-Hall.

Timms, N. 1964: *Social casework*. London: Routledge and Kegan Paul.

Timms, N. and Timms, R. 1977: *Perspectives in social work*. London: Routledge and Kegan Paul.

Titmuss, R. 1970: *The gift relationship*. London: Allen and Unwin.

Index